Calvinism
and Social Problems

CALVINISM
AND SOCIAL PROBLEMS

By

Edward J. Tanis, A M.

Minister, Second Christian Reformed Church,
Englewood, Chicago, Illinois.

WIPF & STOCK · Eugene, Oregon

Wipf and Stock Publishers
199 W 8th Ave, Suite 3
Eugene, OR 97401

Calvinism and Social Problems
By Tanis, Edward J.
ISBN 13: 978-1-62564-263-9
Publication date 8/15/2013
Previously published by Zondervan, 1935

To
My Wife

ACKNOWLEDGMENTS

THE Author's thanks and indebtedness are due *The Presbyterian Tribune* and *The Princeton Theological Review* for several passages cited in his pages, and to the Publishers of the following volumes who have granted him permission to quote certain copyrighted material, in the preparation of his book: *Principles of Economics*, by F. W. Taussig: The Macmillan Company, New York; *John Calvin: The Man and His Ethics*, by Georgia Harkness: Henry Holt and Company, New York, and *Social Pathology*, by John Lewis Gillen: D Appleton—Century Company, New York.

FOREWORD

IN THE autumn of 1934 a number of Christian Reformed ministers met in Holland, Michigan, and organized a general conference for the discussion of the vital problems of our times. It was decided to meet twice a year and to appoint an executive committee to arrange a program. This committee met soon afterwards and requested the writer to furnish a paper for the spring conference of 1935 on American Socialism. The writer was of the opinion that so much had been written on this subject that it could be taken for granted that most of our ministers were familiar with it. Moreover, Dr. Henry J. Ryskamp, Professor of Sociology and Economics in Calvin College, Grand Rapids, Michigan, had just delivered a very scholarly lecture on the subject, "Capitalism, the Socialism of Norman Thomas, and the Christian," so that there was no urgent need of another treatment of this subject. The writer was more interested in a study of Calvin's attitude toward economic questions, and especially in the developments among the Calvinists of the Netherlands in regard to economic and social problems. He suggested a subject along this line and the committee promptly agreed to the change. In the month of May the writer read his paper before a large gathering of Christian Reformed ministers, professors and students, in the auditorium of Calvin Seminary, Grand Rapids. The conference gave the paper a very cordial reception and requested its publication in the near future. The writer preferred to withhold the publication for a while yet, but at the urgent request of many ministers and of the Zondervan Publishing House he consented to prepare it for the press.

The writer does not claim to be an authority on the subject treated in this little book, but it is no secret that he has been deeply interested in social and economic problems for many years, and has taken considerable work in sociology in the University of Chicago. And what means just as much perhaps, he has tried to understand these problems as the members of his beloved congregation struggled with them in their daily lives. As a minister he had to face the economic problem of his own people. The fact is that every minister in these days is compelled to do some thinking and reading about these matters because of the experiences of his parishioners and their lively discussions and debates on unemployment, social insurance, communism, fascism, etc.

To many Christians, and even to many Calvinists, it may seem strange that John Calvin, the great Protestant reformer, was so profoundly interested in the social and economic problems of his age. Most people are ignorant of the significance of John Calvin in the social and political realm. They think of him as a preacher and theologian, and a very cold and austere theologian at that, not realizing that he was a man with wide interests and broad sympathies, a man who carried on an enormous correspondence with the kings and statesmen and religious leaders of Europe. Calvin made a great contribution to the development of the representative form of government. He believed that the laymen should be represented in the government of the church. He created the Presbyterian form of government, and thus helped to provide a pattern for civil governments. He was of the opinion that the safest and most salutary form of government was a government by representative citizens. Thus he helped to lay the foundation of political democracy. That he was deeply interested in economic problems and laid down principles which are valid for all ages will be brought out in the following pages.

The writer does not pretend to offer a final solution of the problems discussed in this book. The ablest economists of our day are not agreed on the solution of these problems. Even the World Economic Conference held in London, June, 1933, was a failure! Even the members of the Supreme Court of the United States do not hold a unanimous opinion as to how far the federal government may interfere in the curbing of economic evils! And even the foremost Dutch Calvinists, Colijn and Anema, do not agree on the details of state supervision in economic matters! But what this writer has tried to do is to make clear what the attitude of Calvin and of some of our modern Calvinists is in regard to some of these problems, and he also attempts to set forth some abiding principles. After all, our first and most urgent need is a knowledge of history and of basic principles. Condemning people as "socialists" does not mean anything. What we need is an intelligent and constructive approach to problems which must be solved if the great abundance of economic goods with which the Creator has blessed us is to be distributed more equitably in our day. There will always be people with more and people with less, but it is contrary to the will of God and also a most dangerous thing if some people have so much that it corrupts them, and others have so little that it prevents them from living a normal human life. Great extremes in wealth and poverty are the sure signs of social decadence. What the Christian people of America need today is an understanding of the evils that beset us in our social life and the earnest desire to remedy them in the light of holy scripture and in the power of the living Lord.

E. J. T.

Englewood,
Chicago, Ill.

CONTENTS

Contents

INTRODUCTORY

OUR DIVINE *Lord taught us to pray, "Give us this day our daily bread." We need bread every day of our life. Without bread we cannot live. Jesus never denied it. "Man shall not live by bread only," he said, but he did not say that we do not live by bread. We all need food, clothing, shelter, and many other blessings for our temporal existence, hence we are in need of an income with which to obtain these things. The bread-butter problem is ever with us.*

The study of the bread-and-butter problem in all its aspects we call economics, or political economy, the adjective political in this case having a social meaning. Political economy, or economics, is the study of how men, living together, making their living, obtain their daily bread. We cannot earn our daily bread alone. We can do so only as members of one body, members of society. A milk strike in Chicago will immediately deprive thousands of babies of their food, and imperil their lives. Our breakfast this morning may have looked very simple, a cereal and a cup of coffee perhaps, but do we realize that thousands of people were engaged in preparing that simple meal for us? The cereal came from the grocer, who must rent a store and hire help to supply us with breakfast food. The grocer must pay taxes and insurance premiums and many other items. And the grocer did not grow our food, but obtained it from the middleman, and this man in turn from the farmer, who at certain seasons of the year employs scores, perhaps hundreds, of men to raise the

grain for our breakfast food. Other men were employed to transport the grain from the farm to the grain
elevator or a shipping center, and from here the food
was carried to the commission houses in Chicago or
New York, and from here again to the millers and the
bakers, or a breakfast food factory. For such a simple
item as the cereal of our breakfast thousands of hands
were needed. And the same is true of the milk and
sugar we put on our cereal or into our coffee. And
the coffee came not merely from the coffee pot heated
by gas, piped in from a gas factory employing hundreds
of men, but perhaps from distant Java, in the Dutch
East Indies, where hundreds of people were laboring
on the coffee plantations. And thus we might continue.
The meat, vegetables, fruits and other items of an ordinary dinner were prepared by an army of men and
women.

And food, of course, is only one item of our "daily
bread." We need clothing, shoes, shelter, and fuel to
keep the house comfortable in winter, and refrigeration
to preserve the food in summer. And money is needed
to insure the house against fire, and an additional sum
is required for taxes for fire and burglary protection.
All this and much more is included in the study of economics, anything but a "dismal science," as somebody
called it. Dr. Thomas Chalmers, the famous evan-
gelical preacher of Scotland, had a better opinion of
it. He wrote two large volumes on the subject, well
spoken of by specialists in the field, and in this work
on economics he urged ministers to interest themselves

in the subject, and to bring the teachings of God's Word to bear on this important phase of our life, lest it become still more ungodly than it already is. This was said one hundred years ago, for the great and saintly Dr. Chalmers died in 1847, and our need of this admonition is so much greater today.

A Christian interest in economics, in the bread and butter problem, is a thing sorely needed today. In spite of our increasing knowledge, and our amazing scientific development, our economic life is not only growing more complex and baffling, but also more irreligious and unethical so that it is becoming harder and harder for a sincere Christian to serve his God while earning his daily bread.

Some well informed men tell us that we are headed for still greater perplexity and confusion. Henry A. Wallace, Secretary of Agriculture, says in his book, "Statesmanship and Religion," (1934), that "we are approaching in the world today one of the most dramatic moments in history," and he warns us that if we do not make the right decision, "the time of the great tribulation is upon us." Dr. E. Stanley Jones, the world-famous missionary, tells us in his latest book, "Christ's Alternative to Communism," that he is "persuaded that Christianity is headed toward a supreme crisis — perhaps a decisive crisis. Events are leading up to a world decision." Dr. Jones' Christian Communism we cannot accept, for we do not believe that it is based upon the Word of God nor upon the best psychological interpretation of man as he is today, but

*his prediction that we are headed for a crisis is worthy
of our serious consideration. Our economic problems
are baffling, and all the more so because we are getting
so far away from the basic teachings of the Word of
God.*

*John Calvin of Geneva was one of the profoundest
interpreters of the Word of God in its application to
all of life, also the economic life. Calvin had a profound insight into the meaning of God's revelation for
all of life. He did not despise the economic life as
the church of the Middle Ages did, but he wanted to
guide it and sanctify it by the light of divine truth.
While he was not a specialist in the field of economics,
he did have something to say about interest on money,
and private property, and taking advantage of working
people in a time of unemployment by paying them low
wages because they are compelled to take this low pay
or starve. Calvin had a good deal to say about these
evils and what he said in Geneva between 1540 and
1564, the year of his death, ought to be thundered into
the ears of men in this year 1935, the four hundredth
anniversary of the publication of the first edition of the
famous "Christian Institutes." In the following pages
we shall examine some Calvinistic declarations in regard to the economic life; briefly survey the modern
developments since 1750; and then attempt to take our
stand in the modern economic life.*

I.

HISTORIC CALVINISM AND ECONOMIC LIFE

Lending Money on Interest.

LENDING MONEY on interest was condemned by the church of the Middle Ages as covetousness and a sin against the eighth commandment, "Thou shalt not steal." Thomas Aquinas, who died in 1274, was the greatest theologian of the medieval church. He took the same position in this matter as the Greek philosopher Aristotle, and also condemned the taking of interest on money. They held that it was wrong to make money with money. Aristotle said that money was to be used as a medium of exchange. Instead of a farmer paying the tailor for his suit with vegetables or grain, he paid him with a sum of money. That was a legitimate use of money, but to use money for the purpose of making more money was unnatural. Aquinas also held this view. And in the Papal indulgences money taken as interest was regarded in the same light as stolen goods. Of course, men did not always live up to this standard. City governments needed money for various projects, and princes and kings needed money for their wars. They could not expect people to lend them this money for nothing. In this case they justified interest on the ground that this was done for the common good. The government existed for the common good, presumably, hence it was no sin to lend money to the government. It was only natural that gradually the practice of charging interest rates became more common, even though frowned upon by many of the more spiritually minded clergy. Down to the days of Luther and Calvin the church officially continued to condemn interest as usury.

In this matter Martin Luther still sided with the Roman Catholic moralists, but John Calvin took an independent position. Calvin made an important distinctionb between money loaned to people in distress, and money loaned for the purpose of doing business at home or carrying on foreign trade. In the one case you are taking advantage of the poor man's plight, but in the other case you are enabling a business man to make a living or even get rich. What wrong can there be in the latter case in charging interest? Nobody thinks it wrong, said Calvin, to ask rent for a farm. You don't let a man use a farm for nothing! He pays rent. Why not? If he did not pay rent, he would have to buy the farm or work for somebody else or starve. Now he leases a farm and pays rent. Everybody approves of this. But suppose that the owner of the farm sells the farm, why does it then become wrong to put that money received for the farm out on interest? The Roman Catholic Church said it was wrong. But Calvin dissented.

To understand this attitude of Calvin, or rather to understand why Calvin differed not only from Rome, but also from Luther on this matter, one must try to see how differently they approached the secular life, man's everyday life, including his economic life. Since the days when the church had allowed certain groups to establish monasteries and convents, the church had come to look upon the religious life as holier than the secular life. A priest was much holier than a farmer or a tailor just because he was a priest. A monk or a nun was holier than a father or mother. The single man was holier than the married man if he remained single with the idea of being holier. Life in the service of the church was holier than life in the world, in the government or in business. Business in particular was looked upon as a *money-making game,* was frowned upon by all pious people. And surely, now that we have gone to the other extreme, a little more of this medieval attitude would not be a bad thing. In the heyday of our prosperity, the seven fat years, 1922-1929, a business man said to the writer that he felt sorry for ministers because people would surely criticize them if they attempted to make an extra dollar, whereas the richer the layman the more men honored him. Well, between this attitude and that of the pious people of the Middle Ages, the latter is certainly to be commended. We give far too much credit, and even honor, to the man who has done nothing more than "make money." But having said this in order not to be misunderstood, it must also be said that the secular life as such is not unholy. A man is not more holy *because* he is a bishop, rather than a merchant or a farmer. So we believe today, but let us not forget that it was John Calvin who taught this to the Christians of these later centuries. Let us honor the man who had the insight and the courage to break with the medieval attitude which condemned all life outside the church as less holy. Let us honor the great Reformer who taught the Protestant church that a God-fearing cobbler is just as holy, and perhaps holier, than any bishop or archbishop. The secular life, including the economic life, is not wicked in itself, said Calvin. A man can serve his God in business just as well as anywhere else. John Wesley was a Calvinist in many of his views, and in a time when England was suffering much from sloth and drunkenness, he said to his followers: "Make all the money you can; save all the money you can; and give all the money you can." Unfortunately many of his followers forgot the third injunction, "Give all the money you can." Wesley had nothing but praise for the energetic business man. And Calvin took the same attitude. Calvin wanted people to be energetic in their daily work. He saw all of life in relation to the sovereign God, and in all of life a man was to serve his God. If he was called to engage in trade, he was to be an energetic trader. Luther was inclined to emphasize the *salvation of the soul*, like many pietists of a later period, but Calvin emphasized the *service of God*. And this service of God was not confined to the church or the monastery, but could be engaged in, in any sphere of life.

Calvin also saw that the economic developments of his time had to be met in a new way. He saw that since the thirteenth century there had been radical changes in the economic life of Europe. The introduction of money on a much larger scale than before, the rise of the credit system, the development of the towns, the increased trade with the nations around the Mediterranean Sea, and the increased facilities for travel had stimulated production and exchange. The wage system was taking the place of the medieval guilds. Money was being invested as never before in textiles, mining and foreign trade. Large financial houses and monopolies were being formed. Many of the people were moving from the farms into the rising towns and hence the middle classes, bourgeoisie, were coming into prominence. The trader, the merchant, the banker were creating new classes, destined to become more influential as the economic development continued. In all these developments money was playing a bigger role all the time. Money was not merely needed as a medium of exchange, but money was needed for the carrying on of business itself, for investments, for expansion, for foreign trade.

For a while the money-changers were Jews, a despised class, but why should all this business be left to the Jews and why should they be allowed to dominate the life of Europe and gradually make the Gentiles their servants? Moreover, the Gentile bishops and Gentile princes needed money, and why should they be under obligation all the time to such a despised class as the murderers of the Lord? So the wealthy Gentiles rationalized, and thus they tried to justify their entrance into the banking business.

To Luther all these new economic developments were baffling. He had rejected the Roman Catholic mass and Mariolatry and purgatory, but that did not mean that he was ready to break with all the medieval traditions. Money-lending for profit was a Jewish game, unworthy of a follower of the lowly Jesus. To use money to make money looked bad to a reformer who had always been a pious monk. Naturally he denounced the new economic developments as being out of the devil. He still held to the position of Aristotle and Aquinas that all interest-taking was sinful. Interest on money was the same thing as the usury condemned in the Bible. Did not Nehemiah condemn usury? "And I was very angry when I heard their cry and these words. Then I consulted with myself, and contended with the nobles and the rulers, and said unto them, Ye exact usury, every one of his brother. And I held a great assembly against them . . . Also I said, The thing that ye do is not good . . . . I pray you, let us leave off this usury." (Nehemiah 5.) And did not the Lord himself say, "Lend, hoping for nothing again?" (Luke 6:35.) Luther felt that he had good authority for denouncing the charging of interest on money.

John Calvin, however, took a new and advanced position, far ahead of that of the church leaders of his day and of an earlier age. Prof. Georgia Harkness in her widely-read book, *John Calvin, the Man and his Ethics*, quotes from a letter to Calvin to Sachinus, written in 1545, in which Calvin discusses the subject of interest at length and he says that "by no testimony of the Scriptures is usury wholly condemned. [By usury he meant interest. T.] For the meaning of the saying of Christ, commonly thought to be very clear, i. e., 'Lend, hoping for nothing again' (Luke 6:35) has been perverted. . . . The words of Christ mean that he commends serving the poor rather than the rich. Thus we do not find all usury forbidden. . . . Now it is said that today, too, usury should be forbidden on the same grounds as among the Jews, since there is a bond of brotherhood among us. To this I reply, that in the civil state there is some difference; for the situation in which the Lord placed the Jews, and many other circumstances, made it easy for them to engage in business among themselves without usury [interest]. Our relationship is not at all the same. Therefore I do not consider that usury is wholly forbidden among us, except it be rejugnant to justice and charity." p. (206.)

In the same connection Calvin said, "I judge that usury must be judged, not by any particular passage of Scripture, but simply by the rules of equity." This indicates that Calvin was far ahead of Luther and the Catholic theologians of the time. He was not afraid to take a new position when changed conditions demanded it. To us this position of the Genevan reformer may seem very simple, because we are so accustomed to thinking of interest on borrowed capital as natural and thoroughly legitimate, but Calvin broke with the historic position of the church in a matter of far-reaching importance for the time and for future economic developments.

At the same time Calvin laid down certain *ethical principles* which were to be observed in regard to the commercial use of money, that is the use of money to make money, such principles as we ought to observe today in our economic life. In plain language Calvin condemned a man who charged poor people for a loan to them in their distress. And he also taught that it was wrong to charge high rates of interest. "One must not go beyond the bounds of equity," said Calvin. And again, "One must not go beyond what the laws of the region permit."

In 1547 a law was passed in Geneva making it unlawful to charge more than five per cent interest per annum. Calvin was in Geneva at the time and he must have approved of this law. In a sermon on Deut. 23:18-20, Calvin speaks of five per cent as a legitimate rate, but he warns against taking this from the poor. The English law at the time allowed a rate as high as ten per cent.

From all this it is evident that Calvin did not condemn the new economic developments as such, but at the same time he was deeply interested in the application of Christian principles to the economic life. No Christian had the right to say that "business is business," or, "religion and business have nothing in common." In business a man had to be a Christian as well as in his church and in his home. A man need not shun the economic life as if it were bad in itself, but he should conduct himself in the economic spheres like a Christian. If he has made his money honestly he may put it out on interest, and make money with his money, but the interest which he charges must be *fair, equitable, in harmony with that which is for the common good*. And seeing that man is by nature selfish and corrupt, and that even the Christian is not perfect, but subject to many temptations, Calvin favored the adoption of laws to safeguard the economic life from unethical practices. All this may sound very simple to some readers, but if these simple principles of Calvin were applied to our whole economic life today, we certainly would not suffer from the evils of capitalism, nor would we be exposed to the menace of half-baked economic theories or radical social experiments. After years of reading and meditation on some of the profoundest problems of life, the writer has come to the conclusion that the things we *must know* for our temporal and eternal well-being are *very simple,* and this is true not only in the sphere of religious philosophy but also in the sphere of our economics. That is not saying that there are no perplexing and baffling situations in life and no profound problems. There certainly are. But what we *must know* in order to "live and die happily" — to borrow the language of the Heidelberg Catechism — has been revealed to us in the Law and in the Gospel. If we walk in this higher light, we shall not stumble, as Christ himself has assured us. He meant just what He said, "I am the light of the world," the light that must also shine into our economic world if we are to have an answer to the prayer he taught us, "Give us this day our daily bread." The prayer will be answered in the measure that we walk in the light of the Gospel. The economic depression of the last few years would never have been so severe, and perhaps it would never have occurred at all, if the leaders and the people had been real Christians like Calvin in their economic life. His motto was, *Coram Deo* — living in the presence of God. "In Thy light we see the light."

Property and Wealth

Calvin not only took a different stand than did the medieval church in regard to interest on money, but he also broke with the medieval religious conception concerning property and wealth. Many of the early church fathers and also of the Medieval Church did not believe it was good for a Christian to have many possessions. The following quotations from articles in *The Princeton Theological Review*, for April and July, 1923, are very interesting in this connection. Says the author: "The renunciation of property, poverty by taking a vow, said the Medieval Church, was the teaching of Christ and the apostles as a way of attaining apostolic perfection. Thus such passages were quoted as Matt. 16:24, 'If any man will come after Me, let him deny himself and take up his cross and follow Me'; and Matt. 19:21, 'If thou wouldest be perfect, go sell what thou hast and give to the poor, and thou shalt have treasure in heaven;' Luke 9:3, 'Take nothing for your journey, neither staves nor scrip, neither bread, neither money; neither have two coats apiece.' The words and example of the apostles they added to these teachings. They 'sold their possessions and goods, and parted them to every man, as every man had need.' 'Our Lord Jesus, though he was rich, yet for your sakes became poor, that through his poverty ye might become rich.' All these passages and many others we find quoted by the Medieval Church as proof that voluntary poverty was such an aid to perfection. . . . Take up the *Vitae Patrum*, the *Acta Sanctorum*, or even *The Dictionary of*

Christian Biography, and at once you feel that here is an adulation of renunciation, especially a renunciation of property. Even modern writers on the apostolic age ... extol the poverty of the early christians, and none can speak of their charity without mentioning also their renunciation." The writer reminds us that Clement, Augustine, and many others praised a life of renunciation as ideal, and he quotes Basil as saying, If any man calleth aught his own he maketh himself a stranger to the elect of God.

Francis of Assisi, founder of the famous Franciscan order, said: "Money, O my brother, is unto the servants of God naught else but the devil and a poisonous serpent." In later times men were wont to say: "The Franciscans, Christ, and the Apostles held no property." Aquinas is quoted as saying, "Though all in general who worship God may be called religious, the name is especially given to such as dedicate their entire lives to the worship of God, keeping aloof from worldly business." Saint Ambrose, under whom the mighty Augustine was converted, said: "Nature produced all things for the common use of all men. Nature produced the common right of property but usurpation the private right." Tertullian, who died A.D. 220, spoke of the giving of alms as "fellowship in property." Some of the church fathers speak of the giving of alms as a matter of *justice* and not of *charity*. Said Gregory the Great, a noble pope who died, 604: "Alms are justice rather than mercy."

The writer in *The Princeton Theological Review* goes on to say: "This principle that almsgiving is an act of justice rather than mercy, is very significant, and forms a very important element in the medieval conception of property. In short, to the Fathers and the Medieval Church the only natural condition is that of common ownership and use. They admit however that human nature being as it is, since the Fall, greedy, avaricious, and vicious, it is impossible for man to live normally under the conditions of common ownership. Private property is therefore practically the creation of the state and is defined, changed, and limited by the state. So they traced from the words of the law, the prophets, the wisdom writers, Christ, the apostles, and the schoolmen a distinction definitely made in the canon law by Gratian in the twelfth century between the law of nature and the positive law [the state] in regard to property. 'By the law of nature,' says Gratian, 'all things are common to all men; and this principle was observed by the Christians in Acts. This principle also was handed down by the philosophers (note the influence of Plato, Seneca and Aristotle here). Actually private property is the creation of the state." And once more Aquinas is quoted: "The temporal goods that heaven bestows on a man are his as to ownership, but as to the use they ought not to be his exclusively, but also should benefit others, who can be maintained out of them."

The consequences of this conception of property are familiar to all who have any acquaintance with the later middle ages. Laziness, vagabondage, mendicancy became all too common. Idleness, rather than industry, was a virtue. Begging for alms instead of working for a living was an act of faith. There appeared the strange paradox of a man trusting in *works* to justify him in the sight of God, and shunning *work* as a thing that was not holy! In the light of this common attitude toward work and property we are now prepared to understand Calvin. He was not a twentieth century capitalist, but a sixteenth century religious and moral reformer who saw the evils of a false asceticism, and naturally put the emphasis on toil and frugality. He urged people to work hard, to appreciate the value of honest toil, to save what they could, to avoid living in profligacy, and to provide for themselves and their families. The result, of course, was the accumulation of property in many instances. Calvin exalted work, praised the man who was thrifty, approved of interest on money, and inevitably some of his followers became rich. A century later we find that the Huguenots were the backbone of the French nation, and among them were most of the successful merchants and manufacturers and bankers. When the Roman Catholic Louis XIV revoked the Edict of Nantes, and drove thousands of Calvinists out of France, he was robbing France of that prosperous middle class that had practiced the teachings of Calvin in its daily vocation.

Calvin believed in private property, and not in communism. In his attack on the Libertines he says: "But, finally, to leave no order among men, they [the Libertines who advocated communism] also make a similar confusion as to goods: saying that it is the communion of saints for no one to possess anything of his own but for each to take whatever he can. At the beginning [of the Reformation] there were some silly Anabaptists who talked this way. But now that such an absurdity has been rejected by all as repugnant to common sense, so that even the original authors are ashamed of it, these libertines have taken refuge in it . . . ." From this it is evident that Calvin did not approve of the communism of his day, which is not saying that he would condemn the public ownership of natural resources. It is conceivable, though by no means certain, that the public ownership of natural resources might mean more personal possessions for a larger number of people. If this public ownership were efficient and honest, this could be the case. Calvin always condemned those monopolies which were contrary to public welfare, as we shall show presently.

Calvin and Exploitation.

In a striking passage in which Calvin ridicules the idea that a man must never leave his vocation, he condemns extortion, business corruption, and the monopolies that oppress the poor. "If a lawyer wants to get fines, if he helps one party oppress the other, if he crushes the good cause to favor the wrong, he is not to blame! For each must follow his vocation. If merchants destroy the world with monopolies, if they counterfeit and disguise their goods, if they perjure themselves every hour to defraud and circumvent, if they plunder and consume all they can snatch, let nobody speak! For that would blaspheme the vocation of the Lord!" This is a satire on the medieval conception of a man's vocation, and at the same time a powerful denunciation of the evils that cursed the economic life of that day. To be sure, there is nothing new under the sun. Human nature is the same throughout all ages. Corruption appears in many forms, but its source is ever the same: the corrupt human heart! "Out of the heart of man proceed evil thoughts," said one who "knew what was in man." (John 2:25.)

Calvin was familiar with the evil of unemployment, and the exploitation of the unemployed. In a sermon on Deut. 24:14-18, he said: "If I compel a poor man to work for me and I pay him only half his wage, it is certain that I defraud him of half his labor ... If I bargain with some one to work for me, and the day's work will cost so much, but then the day's work becomes so much shortened that a poor man having done all he can has not enough to live on, what then? I see that the man has no opportunity to work. He is in my power; I can get him for what I want to pay. That is what the rich often do — they spy out occasions to cut down the wages of the poor by half when they have no employment." These are not the words of a radical New York soap-box orator, but of the profoundest theologian of the Reformation, proof that theological learning and a passion for social justice can go hand in hand. The fact is they ought never to be divorced! True theology is the knowledge of GOD, and there is no knowledge of GOD save in relation to MAN. We do not know God as we ought to know Him, if we do not understand our duty toward God's creature, man. Theology must furnish the principles, and sociology the material for the proper study of human society.

If Calvin were living today he would probably be the theologian with the best insight into human society. How the man would thunder against the exploitation of the unemployed, so common an evil in this long depression! Hear the words as they are hurled from the Cathedral pulpit in Geneva: "That is what the rich often do — they spy out occasions to cut down the wages of the poor by half when they have no employment."

Calvin's commentaries fairly teem with his vigorous denunciations of exploitation. In commenting on the fifteenth psalm he says: "It is also a very strange and shameful thing, that, while all other men obtain the means of their subsistence with much toil . . . . that money-changers should sit at their ease without doing anything, and receive tribute from the labor of all other people. Besides, we know that it is not the rich who are exhausted by their usury, but poor men, who ought rather to be relieved. . . . We see that the end for which the law (the law of God against oppression) was framed, that men should not cruelly oppress the poor, who ought rather to receive sympathy and compassion. This was, indeed, part of the judicial law which God appointed for the Jews in particular; but it is a common principle of justice which extends to all nations and all ages, that we should keep ourselves from plundering and devouring the poor who are in distress and want."

More than seven hundred years before Christ was born the prophet Isaiah condemned the unjust monopolies. "Woe unto them that join house to house, that lay field to field, till there be no room, and ye be made to dwell alone in the midst of the land!" (chap. 5:8.) Says the exegete of Geneva in his exposition of this passage: "Isaiah now reproves their insatiable avarice and covetousness, from which the acts of cheating, injustice, and violence are wont to arise. For it cannot be condemned as a thing in itself wrong, if a man add field to field and house to house; but he looked at the disposition of mind, which cannot at all be satisfied, when once it is inflamed by the desire of gain. So great is the keenness of covetous men that they desire to have everything possessed by themselves alone, and reckon everything that is obtained by others to be something which they want, and which has been taken from them. . . . All the while they do not consider that they need the assistance of others, and that a man left alone can do nothing: all their care is to scrape together as much as they can, and thus they swallow up everything by their covetousness . . . .

"As to the size of houses, the same remark which we made about the fields will apply; for he points out the ambition of those who are desirous to inhabit spacious and magnificent houses. If a man who has a large family makes use of a large house he cannot be blamed for it; but when men, swollen with ambition, make superfluous additions to their houses, only that they may live in greater luxury, and when one person alone occupies a building which might serve for the habitation of many families, this undoubtedly is empty ambition, and ought justly to be blamed. Such persons act as if they had a right to drive out other men, and to be the only persons that enjoyed a house or a roof, and as if other men ought to live in the open air, or must go somewhere else for an abode."

No doubt these words will startle many people who think of Calvin only as a theologian and the teacher of the doctrine of predestination. Calvin was first of all a theologian, a great religious teacher, but a teacher with a profound interest in *real life,* in the crying needs and problems of his age, and he burned with indignation as he saw the rich monopolizing lands and houses. In language so vehement that it ofttimes sounds like that of a modern radical he condemned the exploitation of men and of the God-given sources of human wellbeing. "For what thing could be more base than that they who supply us with bread by their labor, should suffer through want? and yet this monstrous thing is common." (From Calvin'c *Commentary on James,* 5.)

Other Calvinists.

A few brief statements from other Calvinists on this subject will indicate their interest in the application of Christian principles to economic problems. John Knox, who died in 1572, eight years after the death of his great master, John Calvin, was the foremost leader in the Scottish Reformation. In his *Scotch Book of Discipline* he denounces the oppression of the poor by exactions, and also deceiving them in buying and selling. Thomas Cartwright, one of the leading Calvinists in England, expressly declares that if a man is guilty of charging a high rate of interest he may not be admitted to the Lord's Supper. Without changing the spelling peculiar to the times we give this quotation from the *Puritan Manifestoes:* "He that hath usurie proved him, so that he lose his principal for taking above ten in the hundred [ten per cent on a hundred dollars, the rate allowed at the time by English law —T.] yet shall he also, for committing so hanious offense against God and his churches, to the very ill example of others, not be allowed to the sacraments, until he shewe himselfe repentaunt for the faulte and thereby to satisfie the congregation so offended by him." Cartwright believed that the state had the right to legislate in matters of this kind. He knew nothing of that "rugged individualism" of America which ofttimes has been as ruthless as rugged. And in addition he believed that the Church should discipline these ruthless individualists who have no regard for the rights and needs of others.

The Puritans took the same position. Under Cromwell, in 1651, a law was passed forbidding a higher rate of interest than six pounds on a loan of one hundred pounds (six per cent). Cromwell also put through an ordinance for the protection of poor debtors. Richard Baxter, in his famous *Christian Directory*, teaches that all interest on money is sinful if it is in conflict with justice or charity. He holds that the Mosaic law was intended to protect the poor from oppressive contracts and that the principles of the Mosaic law are binding still. Baxter said it was sinful "when you lend for increase where charity obligeth you to lend freely: even as it is sin to lend expecting your own again, when charity obligeth you to give it." Even on *business loans* Baxter condemned the demand for interest if the borrower cannot pay, or if the business does not yield enough profit to pay *full interest.* Baxter contended that interest could not be made the first charge upon industry. It would be hard to apply these principles of Baxter today but the spirit which prompted them was that of love for the neighbor, a profound regard for his well-being. A man might not use his money simply to make *more money,* but rather to provide the necessary funds for business in general *so that all could live.* If a man had so much money that he could put part of it out on interest, there was no need of charging a higher rate than he needed for self-protection. This also shows, by the way, that there were other and nobler motives operative in Calvinism than "make all you can" and "save all you can." Weber and others go too far when they charge Calvinism with being responsible for the evils of modern capitalism.

Richard Baxter also had something to say in regard to *price,* a subject still more involved today when considered in the light of Christian ethics. Baxter puts the question: "How shall the worth of a commodity be judged of?" and he furnishes this answer: 1. "When the law setteth a rate upon anything (as on bread and drink among us) it must be observed. 2. If you go to the market, the market price is much to be observed. 3. If it be an equal contract, with one that is not in want, you may estimate your goods as they cost you, or are worth to you, though it be above the common

price; seeing the buyer is free to take or leave them.
4. But if that which you have to sell be extraordinarily
desirable or worth to some one person more than to
you or to another man, you must not make too great
an advantage of his convenience or desire: but be glad
that you can pleasure him, upon equal, fair and honest
terms. 5. If there be a secret worth in your commodity
which the market will take no notice of (as it is usual
in a horse), it is lawful for you to take according to
the true worth if you can get it. But it is a false rule
of them that think their commodity is worth as much
as any one will give." Baxter is in agreement with
Dr. Ames, another Puritan moralist, who also took the
position that the price determined by the government
was final. Government regulation of price in regard
to the necessaries of life was a thing these men believed
in as necessary for the protection of the common man.
One meets with this price regulation in the matter of
food again and again in history; for example, in the
Babylonian legislation before the days of Moses. H. G.
Wood says: "It is noteworthy, first, that Baxter had no
quarrel with the exercise of public authority to establish a fair price for necessaries, and second, that he
refused to sanction the sacrifice of moral consideration
to the tender mercies of the forces of supply and demand. In both these positions, Baxter is thoroughly
normal. Both Puritans and Anglicans, in the seventeenth century, agreed on these points."

The British scholar just quoted also refers to an
"Act for Advancing and Regulating the Trade of this
Commonwealth," adopted by the Puritans, who were

then in power, in August, 1651, and, according to the Preamble, passed 'to the end that ye poore people of this land may be set on work and their Families preserved from beggardie and ruine ... and no occasion left for either Idleness or Poverty.' The phrase 'to set the poore on work' is the regular phrase for the relief of the unemployed, and it links the aim of the Commonwealth government with the best traditions of the Privy Council." For the government to provide work in times of distress was regarded as a normal thing.

The Puritans were also down on monopolies. We find that in the first year of the Puritan Commonwealth, the government attorney was directed to prosecute a corn monopolist at Ipswich, "so that the poore people may see that care is taken of them in time of dearth." Later in the same year, a warrant was issued against Samuel Truelove of Wapping, and Mr. Bucknell, shipmaster, to "attend the Council to answer as to a combination for raising the price of coals." This step was followed by the appointment of a committee "to consider how the price of coal for the poor may be brought down, to confer with the Lord Mayor and to prepare an act." The general principle guiding such action is laid down in a memorable sentence in Cromwell's famous dispatch to parliament concerning the Dunbar fight: "Be pleased to reform the abuses of all professions: and if there be anyone who makes many poor to make a few rich, that suits not a Commonwealth."

The Puritans, like all other good Calvinists, regarded life as a stewardship, hence we are to find a work, said Baxter in his *Christian Directory*, in which we are "serviceable to God and the common good." Baxter also "warns men against imposing oppressive rents, against oppressing laborers by withholding wages, and against imposing oppressive conditions of labor, especially combinations which render men unfit for or careless of their religious duties." The Puritans were certainly interested in fair wages and good working conditions, and that not merely from a secular and earthly point of view, but because of men's spiritual needs. The Puritans taught very definitely that no man is an absolute owner of anything, but all things belong to God, and whatever we possess must be used for the common good. Hence oppressive monopolies are wicked in the sight of God and should be restrained or destroyed by the government. The best men in the Anglican Church (the Episcopal state church), who were also Calvinists, held the very same views. The Calvinists were deeply conscious of man's social responsibility. Their religion was ethical and practical, and they held that no man could say that he loved God if he did not love his neighbor and deal justly.

We can summarize the economic principles of Calvin and his followers in these statements:

1. Calvinists did not believe that the consecrated child of God should shun the economic life, much less look upon it with contempt.

2. They believed it was right to go into business or industry for profit, and with their money to make more money. They believed in the profit motive, in financial investments, foreign trade.

3. They rejected communism and believed in pri-

vate property. They did not believe that God intended that all wealth should be equally distributed.

4. They laid great emphasis on industry, thrift, frugality, and sobriety, and moderation in all things.

5. All life was regarded as a stewardship, and property and other possessions were held in trust for God. Property might be owned by the individual, but it was to be used for the good of all. Calvin condemned the man who hoarded his money instead of investing it, and making it profitable, and with the profits serving society.

6. Dishonesty in all forms, extortion, the oppression of the poor, monopolies especially of the resources of life, taking advantge of labor in a time of unemployment, the payment of low wages when higher wages could be paid, were abuses definitely condemned by Calvin and his followers.

7. Government control in regard to economic matters, whenever necessary, was advocated by the Calvinists. In Calvin's time already Geneva regulated the rate of interest, and in the time of the Puritans prices were regulated in regard to some of the necessaries of life for the protection of the poor. Monopolies and other abuses were punished by the government.

Did Calvinism Create Modern Capitalism?

Some modern writers are of the opinion that the influence of Calvinism on our economic system has been so great that it must be held responsible for the characteristic features of modern capitalism. In 1905 Weber of Germany published his *Protestant Ethic and the Spirit of Capitalism* and developed the thesis that the Calvinistic emphasis on the significance of work, and on such virtues as thrift and frugality, had contributed enormously to the growth of capitalism. Later investigators have pointed out that there is considerable overstatement in this thesis. Prof. Georgia Harkness in her book, *John Calvin, the Man and his Ethics,* says: "I believe that he has overstated his case. Capitalism existed both in form and spirit before Calvin's day. As Brentano, Sombart, and Tawney have pointed out, economic forces outside the stream of religion contributed to its growth before the Reformation. . . . The development of capitalism in England and Holland was due in large measure to economic causes, particularly the territorial discoveries and the opening up of new lands to colonization and trade. Religious and economic factors were so intertwined that it is impossible to say categorically that either produced the other."

I have discussed this subject with Dr. John T. McNeill and Dr. Wm. Pauck of the University of Chicago, who are authorities on the period of the Reformation, and they reject the proposition that modern capitalism is the child of Calvinism.

We must also remember that it is especially within the last one hundred and fifty years that the economic system has undergone great changes, and within this period Calvinism has ceased to dominate the cultural life of Europe and America. The Calvinistic emphasis on the ethical aspects of the economic life, man's stewardship and responsibility to God, his duty toward his neighbor, especially the weaker members of society, the sin of extortion and unfair monopolies, all this has been lost sight of in the modern economic struggle. We can honestly acquit Calvinism of having been responsible for man's inhumanity to man in the modern economic life. If the basic religious and moral principles of John Calvin and his truly spiritual descendants had dominated the life of the modern world, we would look upon a different scene today. We would find that the abundance produced by modern machinery would be more equitably (I do not say equally) distributed; that all who are willing to work would have work, and that every honest worker would make a living wage. Calvin would be the last man in the world to curtail production in order to feed the unemployed. On the contrary he would say that every human being must be productive, and he would let all produce, and then distribute the products according to human need.

It is not Calvinism that is responsible for the present economic crisis. Let us see, then, what has happened since Calvinism ceased to be as dominant as it was in the seventeenth century.

II.

THE MODERN ECONOMIC DEVELOPMENTS

Inventions

IN THE eighteenth century men with technical minds and technical interests began to wrestle with the problem of increasing their production. They realized that if machines were invented the output of man's toil could be vastly increased and there would be a greater abundance at a lower price. And the result was that in the eighteenth century several important machines were invented. The first steam engine was invented in 1710, and by 1776 Watt had perfected it so that it would use less coal and be much cheaper to operate. In 1782 it was applied to work machines and to create the blast for the new iron furnaces. Several machines were invented for spinning and weaving, and such names as Hargreaves, Arkwright, Eli Whitney are familiar to all of us. The result was an enormous increase in the production of cotton. Hand spinning disappeared in the cotton and woollen endustry by 1820. Steamboats were successful by 1810, and steam locomotives by 1830, which meant a tremendous revolution in the world's method of transportation. The new machines altered the old processes of production and transportation and profoundly affected man and his whole life, also his social and religious life. Machinery enlarged his power to produce, and the new transportation increased his mobility. A revolution of ideas was also bound to accompany such far-reaching changes in the physical world. It is no wonder that men dreamed of "liberty and equality" and that the philosophy of individualism became so popular in the nineteenth century. It looked as if man had entered a new world, and for any one willing to work there would be a great abundance.

But these great changes were accompanied with bitter disappointments. The Industrial Revolution stimulated the growth of towns, and in the new industrial towns houses were constructed very hurriedly and there were no regulations to prevent over-crowding or cellar dwellings. There were no arrangements for disposing of house refuse. There was no system of drainage and no system of sanitation. The piling up of populations in new areas created filth and diseases so that thousands of people died of smallpox, typhoid fever and cholera.

The introduction of machinery also produced a new type of worker. The old-fashioned handicraftsman was soon beaten in the race by the new competitor, the engine, the machine, which could turn out twenty or a hundred times his output at infinitely less cost. A large proportion of the new factory workers were women and children, who could work for lower wages than the men with families. This gave the masters and the mill-owners a great advantage and they were not slow to take it. Many of them showed neither mercy nor consideration to their hordes of employes. Fur-

thermore, the workshops were foul, damp and unsani-
tary. The working-hours were intolerably long — four-
teen, eighteen, and in some cases twenty hours a day.
The pay, even for men, was miserably low. The cot-
tages were over-crowded, bare and comfortless. The
family life was ruined by the grim necessity of send-
ing out the children to earn wages almost as soon as
they could walk. Robinson, the historian, says that
"the conditions of life in these hideous factory towns
of northern and central England were a scandal which
cried shame upon the richest and most prosperous country in the world."

The workers began to protest against these horrible
conditions so common in the early nineteenth century,
and to form associations for their protection. But
a law was passed in 1799 — the so-called "Combination Law" — which made it a crime for workmen to
confer in regard to wages and conditions, and viola-
tion of the law was punishable by imprisonment or hard
labor for two months. It was Thomas Chalmers, the
great Calvinistic churchman of Scotland, who condemned this law, saying, "It seems altogether fair that
each should make as much as he can of his own labor;
and that just as dealers of the same description meet
and hold consultations for the purpose of enhancing
the price of their commodity, so it should be equally
competent for workmen to deliberate, and fix on any
common, if it be not a criminal agreement, and that
to enhance, if they can, the price of their services.
There really is nothing morally wrong in all this." This
was the progressive and sensible opinion of a *Calvinist,*

but it was not until the year 1924 — a quarter of a
century later — that this unjust law was revoked.

These few facts from the early history of the modern industrial revolution indicate that the so-called machine age was accompanied with misery and injustice
for the working classes. Gradually, however, their associations for the improvement of their conditions were
recognized by law, and a vast amount of social legislation in England and on the continent improved the conditions of the masses so that they actually began to
profit from the new machinery and the increased production.

Other Factors.

But in spite of all the social progress of the nineteenth century, there are many other important factors
in our modern economic development which have created unsatisfactory conditions, so much so that we are
now in the midst of a most serious economic crisis.
The work which was done a hundred and fifty years
ago in the home and on the farm has been carried out
of the home into the factory and is done by men and
women working next to one another, competing with
one another, and creating new psychological and social
situations unknown in the old agricultural economy. In
the old economy there was plenty of work for the
women *in the home*, canning and preserving foods for
the coming year, making clothing, sometimes for most
of the members of the family. In our day women by
the million have followed their work out of the home
into the factory. In many cases they work for less

wages than the men, and put the men out of work. It is nothing uncommon in our day to find a wife and mother in a factory or store or office, and the husband and father taking care of the home!

Another important result of the industrial revolution is that the workers have been divorced from the instruments of production. Before the advent of modern machinery the tailor and shoemaker made their own product from start to finish, regulated their own prices and hours, but the tailor of today, for the most part, is but one worker among ten thousand others, a cog in a vast machine. He does not own the place where he works nor the tools with which he works. He has nothing but his labor, which he must sell in a highly competitive market, and when the labor market is glutted his wages go down, irrespective of the size of his family and his needs, and irrespective of the intrinsic value of his labor. The principle enunciated by Christ that the laborer is worthy of his hire, is mocked at in an age when the rise and fall of the market and the return promised dividend-holders, and other factors, determine the size of the wage. The individual workman today is helpless, absolutely impotent, over against the groups that own the instruments of production and distribution, and he has no way of defending himself except by means of cooperation with his fellows.

Modern machinery and the creation of new methods of finance, the international credit system through international banking, have also exercised a profound influence on our economic life. We no longer produce for actual consumption alone, for actual needs, in a home market, but our modern industrialists and merchants are producing and distributing for a *world market* in which all modern nations become keen and ofttimes unscrupulous competitors. If German merchants can sell cheaper goods in South America than the American, then the factory workers of America are laid off by the thousands and their families are compelled to live on the verge of starvation. No one individual is to blame for such a situation, and in all probability the German *entrepreneur* does not feel that he has been guilty of an unethical act. His workers could work more cheaply than could the American workers, hence he could sell more cheaply, and he took the market away from the American merchant and manufacturer. But whether ethical or unethical, the American laborer and his family suffer from the things that happen in the world market. Just how such a situation is to be remedied is not easy to say. The introduction of socialism or communism in America without the introduction of the new order in all nations, would not remedy the foregoing situation, unless the socialist nation should withdraw from the world market and produce only for home consumption. The world market in our modern life is an economic factor of tremendous importance.

Dangerous Extremes.

Another result of mass production and modern methods of finance is the enormous concentration of wealth accompanied with widespread poverty, or conditions not so far removed from poverty. There have always been rich and poor, and always will be.   An equal distribution of economic goods is not possible and is not even desirable.   If all the wealth of the world were equally divided among the inhabitants on a certain Saturday night, there would have to be another distribution by the next Saturday night, as some people are much better spenders than savers.   Some people can make a dollar go twice as far as others can.   Some people need much more than others.   An equal distribution of wealth would be absurd even if it were possible.   But one of the outstanding characteristics of our age is *the shrinking of the big middle class*, with most of the middle class descending into the proletariat, the group that owns nothing but children, and a very few of the middle class rising into that small group in which the economic wealth, hence also economic and political power, is so enormously concentrated.   This is a bad sign and an unwholesome situation.   The soundest condtion for a nation is to have a big middle-class, owning a home and a little ground, and with enough laid away to provide for the proverbial rainy day.   But that class is continually shrinking in America, especially in the metropolitan areas.   Most of the people in New York and Chicago don't own anything beyond their clothing and furniture.

Here are some interesting facts from reliable sources.   The distribution of wealth in the United States in 1915 was as follows:

The rich, two per cent of the nation, owned sixty per cent of the wealth.

The middle class, thirty-three per cent of the nation, owned thirty-five per cent of the wealth.

The poor, sixty-five per cent of the nation, owned five per cent of the wealth.

Now see what happened between 1915 and 1929 (less than fifteen yrs.):

One per cent of the people owned fifty-nine per cent of the wealth in 1929.

Twelve per cent of the people owned thirty-one per cent of the wealth.

Eighty-seven per cent of the people owned ten per cent of the wealth.

You can also express the distribution of our wealth in the following figures:

1,220,000 individuals own 236 billion dollars, or $111,475 per capita.

14,640,000 individuals own 124 billion dollars, or $8,493 per capita.

106,140,000 individuals own forty billion dollars, or $377 per capita.

These figures, quoted from Mangold, *Social Pathology*, are based on the estimates of wealth for 1930.

These figures do not indicate how large a proportion of the population is entirely without any property.

The Federal Trade Commission also revealed the following facts in regard to the control and ownership of our natural resources. In 1922 six companies controlled a third of the total developed water power; eight companies controlled three quarters of the anthracite coal reserves; 30 companies, more than one third of the soft coal reserves; four companies controlled nearly one half of the copper reservs, and thirty companies controlled over twelve per cent of the petroleum. The listed value of corporate wealth was given as $102,-000,000,000 (one hundred and two billions).

Consider also these facts: the 27,100,000 wage earners in this country own 4.3 per cent of the property; the 6,385,000 farmers own 17 per cent of the property. On the other hand, the 260,000 people having an income of $10,000 or more own 42.5 per cent of the property.

We are all familiar with the enormous amount of profiteering in this country during the war. As a result the number of millionaires increased enormously. In 1914 there were 7,500 millionaires in the United States; in 1917 this number had increased to 19,000, and in 1928 there were 43,000. No doubt there has been some shrinkage in this number. On the other hand, it must be remembered that even during the depression the number of people with an income of more than $10,000 actually increased, whereas we all know what happened to the incomes of the majority of the people during this same period.

Perhaps this is the most serious fact of all in this whole economic situation, namely, that a small class of people profited from the depression, growing fabulously rich, whereas multitudes of people had to live on a dole, and a very large group in the middle class, industrious and thrifty people, lost the savings of many years and are now compelled to live from hand to mouth. There was a time when we could boast of the fact that the industrious man could make a good living and the thrifty person could save for old age, but during the last twenty years that situation has been changed, and today we have multitudes of people without any economic security. If their income stops, they are dependent upon charity. If they are old their savings are gone, and although able to work no one will employ them. The depression made this situation worse, but the situation was here already ever since the outbreak of the world war twenty years ago.

Another serious feature of our industrialized age is that improved machinery continually throws men out of work, men who are less than fifty years, and other industries will not employ them because they are said to be "too old." "Young men" are wanted, that is, men who are not much over thirty years. *I do not mean to say that most of our unemployment is due to machinery, as some contend.* The millions of men displaced by the new farm machinery have been absorbed in new industries which did not exist in 1890. I do not think that new machinery is the biggest cause of unemployment. But what happens is that when the older men are laid off other firms refuse to take them on because they prefer to break in the younger men. In other words, there is far less mobility in labor than there used to be, and that works a hardship on multitudes of men and their families, men who are by no means fifty years old.

Characteristics of Modern Economic Life.

In a good description of the things characteristic of our modern economic order, Dr. H. J. Ryskamp of

Calvin College says: "Under Capitalism, in its unique development, men who can bring together large sums of money, produce goods with the use of machinery with hired labor, largely for the market, and for a profit. It is a system that involves concentration of production, standardization, the wage system, scientific management — and that is guided almost altogether by price. It is a system that with its emphasis on production for an impersonal market, and for a profit, has produced new problems in the relation between capital and labor, that in a new way has involved us in the excesses of nationalism and war . . . Capitalism is unique in its methods of production, particularly in its tendency toward mechanization and standardization; in its reliance upon new forms of property and upon the huge concentration of wealth in these forms of property; in its production for a vast and unknown market; in its being regulated not directly by human forces but indirectly by these through the medium of price; in the impersonal character of the relation between those engaged in production; and in the intensification of selfishness that has been encouraged by this combination of factors." *Capitalism, the Socialism of Norman Thomas, and the Christian,* (Sept. 1934.) This is a very accurate and concise description of our modern economic order. It is based upon such facts as any intelligent man can see for himself. *But it is very important that we should see these facts. Our present economic order is different from that of any previous period of history, certainly different from that which was known to men in Bible times.* The beginning of this modern development could be seen in Calvin's day, but Calvin certainly could not foresee what has come to pass in the last two hundred years and especially in the last fifty years.

Sombart, Weber and others have tried to summarize the dominant ideas in our economic order. Sombart says that Capitalism is characterized by three ideas: *"acquisition, competition,* and *rationality.* The first idea is that of *acquisition.* Capitalism is motivated by the desire for profit. Hope of profit is the very soul of the system. No matter how large the profits, they can never reach a level sufficient to satisfy the spirit of capitalism. Seeing that in the pre-capitalistic system, goods were produced and traded so that consumers' needs might be supplied [important statement — T.] and that ample livelihood for producers and merchants might be provided, economic processes were grounded in personal values. Human relationships were the touchstone governing economic transactions. Not so in the capitalistic system, where acquisition is the aim of all economic activity. The aim of the system is not the welfare of people nor of any individual, but an increasing stock of material things and a greater variety of services."

In the second place, "Competition characterizes the attitudes shown in the processes of acquisition. Under this system acquisition must be free from regulation by means of bonds imposed upon the individual from the outside, and from any limit placed upon the amounts which the individual may acquire. The individual insists upon freedom to seek his profits without interference and in accordance with his own natural abilities. He takes great risks of failure, but also great chances of success. The only limit upon his activity is a penal code. The result is that all other values except that of profits must be subordinated. Ruthlessly capitalism with its goal of profits ignores the value of human personality and the concepts of the general welfare. Not only does the desire for profits dominate the economic field, but it reaches over into the cultural fields of human society and tends to set up its own values in those fields. A human being is no longer looked upon as of any value in himself; he is merely a unit of labor power. Nature itself is no longer a thing of beauty, with values of its own for human beings, but is a reservoir of materials and forces to assist the making of gain. Hence the appalling unscrupulousness and ruthlessness of modern business.

" In the third place, capitalism is characterized by *rationality*. By that we mean a tendency to long-range planning, careful consideration of the adaptation of means to ends, and cold and careful calculation of what measures will bring the greatest gain. It is this characteristic which has brought into such prominence in modern business the highly developed system of cost accounting, efficiency plans, experts, and the careful and manifold functionalization of business organizations. It also accounts for the introduction of modern technology into industry and commerce, and the departmentalization and coordination of the parts of the whole organization. It has given rise to modern methods of salesmanship and the development of new forms of retailing." (Quoted from *Social Pathology*, by John Lewis Gillen, p. 451 ff.)

"In the period of what Sombart calls full capitalism which began about 1750 and closed in 1914 with the outbreak of the World War, the inherent tendencies of the capitalist system came to their full expression. Struggle for profits and what he calls economic rationalism, completely controlled and molded all economic relationships. In this period economic activity enlarged demands of business. Plans were introduced to make business more productive and industry everywhere was mechanized. Institutionalized rather than personal relationships existed between employer and employed. Business was organized from top to bottom in a strict regimentation. Buyer and seller no longer came face to face, but the process of exchange was mechanized as far as possible on the basis of fixed prices. Merchandise was increasingly standardized, corporate systems took the place of the old personal relationships. Credit institutions, tending to operate impersonally, everywhere arose. Corporate control took the place of individual ownership and partner ownership. Large financial concerns grew up to provide credit for the large units of industry. Credit instruments of all sorts, like bonds and certificates of stock, took the place of personal notes, and again impersonal supplanted personal relationships. Wall street and Lombard Street tended to dominate the whole industrial system through their power over credit." Quoted from *Social Pathology*, by John Lewis Gillen, p. 451 ff.)

This, then, is our modern economic system under which we live, and in which every human being is deeply involved. And the most important fact of all perhaps is this that the system has given the natural man so much opportunity to reveal the worst side of his corrupt nature. It is a system in which it is so easy to do wrong without suffering the consequences of our wrongdoing. The retail merchant who cheats his customers is soon discovered, but the corporation that exhorts money from a long-suffering public can do so with impunity. There is good reason for speaking of "soulless corporations."

The prophetic picture of Babylon's downfall in Revelation 18 implies a severe condemnation of the economic life of the last days. How near we are to the realization of that picture no man knows, but how true it is that in the economic life of our day souls are sacrificed for dollars! How true that human life is sacrificed all the time on the altar of selfishness and greed, and to satisfy the lust for wealth and for the social and political power that goes with wealth! Philip Mauro, in his book, *The Number of Man*, written as long ago as 1909, says: "Everyone of the colossal fortunes of the day exists because of the impoverishment of many whose labor has gone to the production of the wealth that constitutes them. Business principles are frankly the quintessence of selfishness . . ." Any one who knows anything at all about our modern economic life knows that for the most part, and making allowance for noble individuals who are an exception, this life is thoroughly ungodly. The pulpit ofttimes condemns science as "ungodly," but there is far more of the altruistic spirit in science than in business and industry. Science at least attempts to minister to the bodies of men, but the modern world of industry and business only too often crushes the life out of men. It is a struggle so ruthless and brutal that only the fittest survive.

III.

TWENTIETH-CENTURY CALVINISM AND MODERN LIFE

WHAT SHOULD our attitude as twentieth century Calvinists be in the midst of these economic developments, especially in view of the fact that the lofty ethical principles of John Calvin are shamefully disregarded, in the present economic order?

In the first place, we must realize that we are facing totally new conditions. Our economic life is different from that which Calvin faced and to which he applied his more liberal interpretations of the Scripture, I mean more liberal as compared with those of the medieval church and of Luther. Machinery and mass production, with production for a foreign market, and the whole economic life dominated by the profit motive, was unknown in Calvin's day. Sombart is right when he says that *our* economic life is dominated by *acquisition, competition,* and *rationality,* and this was not the case in the sixteenth century. We can be certain, in view of this fact, that Calvin would not approve of the profit motive *as it dominates our modern economic life.* In view of his own exalted conception of the relation of human life to God, and to the kingdom of God, he could not approve of an economic life governed solely by the spirit of acquisition and of competition. Even if he did not insist on the removal of the profit motive altogether, he certainly would demand

59

that its operation be placed on an ethical basis.

Secondly, we must remember that we are heirs to a great extent of nineteenth century individualism. We are all subject to the influences of our environment and the spirit of the age, and we have unconsciously imbibed much of the nineteenth century individualism, with the emphasis on individual rights and personal materialistic success. Especially the American pioneer was glad to escape the restrictions of the old world, and here in the new world make his own way, and achieve material success regardless of the rights of his fellowmen. The American hero was the poor boy who had made a fortune out of oil or steel or railroads. That the millionaires had climbed to success on the backs of a hundred thousand under-paid Yankees and foreigners was oftimes lost sight of. Furthermore, in our whole attitude toward life we were individualists, with very little, if any, sense of social responsibility. The spirit of Cain, "Am I my brother's keeper?" was only too often the spirit of America.

We have a splendid illustration of the spirit in the opposition to workmen's compensation, now the law in forty-four states. Before we had the workmen's compensation law, the injured workman, or the family of the workman killed in an industrial accident, had to look out for themselves. They could sue the company, but the litigation was too expensive. The majority of mine operators and owners of factories refused to install safety devices on their machinery until forced by law. Today we have workmen's compensation laws, liability insurance, and safety devices. But for years this valuable social reform, in the interest of the worker and his family, was opposed in the courts and the press as being "socialistic," "paternalistic" and contrary to constitutional rights. Let us not forget that under the influence of this individualism we are apt to take the same attitude toward other necessary social reforms, and instead of acting in the spirit of John Calvin, with all his emphasis on stewardship, we practice the evolution doctrine of the nineteenth century, the doctrine of the survival of the fittest. Never should we forget that nineteenth century individualism had much more in common with Darwinism than with alvinism.

Calvinism is a philosophy of life with a profound appreciation of the organic unity of the human race. Calvin himself was born and raised in the Roman Catholic Church, and this Church built up the greatest social organization the world ever saw. The papacy, the monasteries, the relation of the church to the state and to society, *all this implied a social conception of human life.* And neither Calvin nor Luther ever abandoned the principle of racial solidarity and social unity. Especially Calvin's conception of mankind as fallen in Adam, his doctrine of original sin, of Christ as the Federal Head in the covenant of grace, of the communion of saints, all this made it impossible for Calvin to be an individualist after the pattern of Adam Smith and the Manchester school of political economists. It is no wonder that Calvin was deeply interested in economic problems, in the political and social reforms of Geneva, and that, as Colijn reminds us, he developed a scheme for a municipal weaving factory in

Geneva which was intended to supply work to the unemployed. How many people, even the so-called
educated of our day, think of Calvin as a social reformer?

The fundamental principle of Calvinism is the
sovereignty of God, as Dr. Henry Meeter has clearly
pointed out in his well known book on Calvinism. And
the corollary of that basic principle is *the stewardship
of man*, a truth that Calvin always emphasized but
that we so often forget. Calvin's personal motto,
Coram Deo, implied that he was deeply conscious
of his own stewardship. According to the Genevan reformer, every man is a steward of his talents, time,
possessions, of his capital or of his labor, whatsoever
it may be. No man is sovereign. God alone is sovereign and we are stewards.

And these two principles, the sovereignty of God
and the stewardship of man, Calvin applied to the
economic life.

And it is these two principles which the Antirevolutionary party of the Netherlands, under the leadership of such men as Groen Van Prinsterer, Abraham
Kuyper, Henry Colijn, is applying to the social and
economic problems of the Netherlands, problems which
today are essentially the same as our problems. If
we would see Calvinism at work in the social and political and economic order, we must visit the Netherlands, a privilege this writer has never enjoyed. A historian by the name of Groen Van Prinsterer organized a
Christian political party in that country about one
hundred years ago. Under the leadership of Dr. Abra-

ham Kuyper, first a liberal in his theology, but later
an ardent Calvinist, the party began to make real head-
way until Dr. Kuyper himself became Prime Minister
in 1901. During the last thirty years, with varying
fortunes, the party has continued to function in the political life of the Netherlands, and at the present time
another outstanding leader of the party, Dr. Hendrik
Colijn, is at the head of the government. Dr. Colijn
is a life-long economist, a Calvinist in the true sense
of the word, and deeply interested in the happy solution of social and economic problems. True to his
Calvinism, he is interested in *all* groups, in *all* classes,
and believes that the application of Christian principles to social problems and the *harmonious cooperation*
of all groups and parties in the social order is the only
way out of the present crisis and the surest way in
which to promote national prosperity. Colijn is loyal
to the spirit and principles of the late Dr. Abraham
Kuyper and one who knows no higher honor than to
be a devoted servant of Christ. He sincerely believes
that in Christianity lies the solution of our economic
and social problems. Of course, almost thirty years
have elapsed since Kuyper did his greatest work, and
it is no wonder that a man like Colijn puts far more
emphasis on social reform and social legislation than
did Kuyper. The times have changed greatly, problems have multiplied and grown more acute and complex, and Colijn is far more interested in governmental
control and regulation than was his party a generation
ago.

This is brought out very clearly in the new edition

of the party's platform, which fills a book of six hundred pages and is a comprehensive statement of the principles and program of the *Antirevolutionary* party of the Netherlands. The name *Antirevolutionary* indicates that the party is opposed to the revolutionary spirit of the French revolution and of modern communism. It is also opposed to *socialism* inso far as socialism fails to reckon with the sinfulness of man and ignores the teachings of Holy Scripture for our secular life. The party sometimes cooperates with the socialists in the Holland parliament in obtaining such social legislation as sickness and unemployment insurance, but it is positively opposed to the spirit and principles of socialism as a system. The party believes in social justice, but it does not believe that we can create a perfect world. The Antirevolutionary party has an *eschatological conception of history* and holds that the present history of the world will end in a *crisis*. But at the same time every good Calvinist believes that he has a duty toward his environment, his community, toward the society of which he is a member for the time being. He must be "the light of the world" and "the salt of the earth." He must shed the light of Scripture upon social and economic problems and by virtue of his religious life and spiritual influence he must restrain the corruption inherent in human life. Dr. Robert Hutchins, president of the University of Chicago, said in his commencement address, June, 1935, that "the worst thing about life is that it is demoralizing." The Calvinist believes that Christianity is the greatest force in resisting and overcoming this demoralization, and that Christianity must make itself felt in the social and economic and political life. Hence Christianity must apply itself to social problems. Fifty years ago, says Colijn, Abraham Kuyper already saw the need of social legislation. Kuyper was ahead of his party ofttimes. In his monumental exposition of the principles and program of the Antirevolutionary part, Dr. Colijn reminds his readers that as long ago as 1874, Dr. Kuyper, who was the coming leader of the party, in a maiden speech in the Dutch parliament, pleaded with great ability for extensive labor legislation. Colijn says that while men may differ as to how far the government should go in regulating the ecomonic life, we are all agreed that it is obliged to provide social legislation. We must give the Antirevolutionary party credit, he says, for having cooperated vigorously in securing the passage of social legislation. WhatColijn says is very true, as we all know or can know, but we might add that Calvinists of the Netherlands have advocated social laws still condemned in America as "socialistic." (*Toelichting*, etc. p. 375.)

Speaking of conditions among the Jews in Old Testament times, Colijn says: "The prophets of the Lord were not coldly indifferent to the social needs of their times. They pointed the people to abnormal conditions and in the name of the Lord they called upon the nation to practice righteousness and justice. (*Toelichting*, etc. p. 377.)

In condemning the individualism of Adam Smith, the Manchester school of political economy, and of the French Revolutionists, Colijn writes: "Our social dis-

tress is largely the result of a false individualism which
was exalted in the French revolution. Due to the influence of liberal principles in politics the duty of the
state in regard to social problems was ignored. And
the thing that worked untold harm was the destruction
of personal faith, and of the sense of responsibility to
God in the sphere of the economic life." (*Toelichting
op het Antirevolutionair Beginselprogram,* p. 384.)

Dr. Colijn lays, great stress upon *social responsibility*. In his vigorous style he declares very emphat-
ically that both the Old and the New Testament proclaim the truth of the organic character of human life,
using the figure of the one body with its many members.
The covenant conception, which represents mankind as
fallen in Adam but redeemed in Christ, the doctrine of
original sin, but no less the doctrine of God's covenant
with the believers and their offspring — this profound
Biblical conception is based upon an organic view of
humanity. In this conception men are not merely so
many individuals, but they are *members of the one
body* . . . The gospel of Christ proclaims the equality
of all men before God; it binds men together without
ignoring their differences; it creates peace; it supresses
egoism; it summons all men in all things to be well-
pleasing unto God, also in those things which pertain
to labor and industry. It honors personality, but no
less does it acknowledge the significance of the social
order. Our life in the state and in society, as Kuyper
taught us years ago, is a school of preparation for a
higher social life in the glorious kingdom of God. In
living the Christian life with our fellowmen we prepare

ourselves for the perfect social life of the kingdom of heaven. (*Toelichting*, etc. p. 406.)

Much more might be quoted and really ought to be quoted from that magnificent treatise of Dr. Colijn in which the Calvinistic principles are applied to social and economic problems. Here we have a Calvinism so little understood and appreciated in the modern world, and yet so full of promise if seriously applied to our difficult problems. Even so many Christian Reformed people, descendants of pious Calvinists of the nineteenth century, and so many Presbyterians, sons and daughters of Calvinists who made Scotland great and famous, do not know what a comprehensive philosophy of life is offered to the world in Calvinism. They do not realize that Calvinism teaches the solidarity of the human race, the organic nature of human society, the equality of all men before God, the responsibility of all the members, and especially of the most highly favored, toward all the other members in the social body. Just because Calvinism emphasizes the sovereignty of God it is bound to emphasize also the *stewardship* of man. God is the Creator of all men, hence no respecter of persons. All are duty bound to serve Him and to serve humanity. The greed and selfishness and acquisitive spirit, so characteristic of our present social order, is contrary to the law of God and in conflict with the organic nature of society. God hath made of one blood all the children of men, hence there ought to be a consciousness of social duty and social obligation. All this is emphasized in Calvinism. And it is this Calvinism which passed through a remarkable revival in the

Netherlands in the nineteenth century, and is still bearing fruit under the leadership of men like Dr. Hendrik Colijn and the late A. W. F. Idenburg.

This Calvinistic emphasis on social responsibility should not be confused with the so-called "social gospel." The "social gospel" is largely the offspring of Ritschlianism, a German-made brand of nineteenth century theology which taught the Fatherhood of God and the brotherhood of man, without due recognition of the enormous strain placed upon this fatherhood and brotherhood by the sin of man. Calvinism takes sin far more seriously than did Ritschl and his followers. Sin is alienation from God, accompanied with hatred toward God and man, so that there is need of a supernatural atonement and supernatural regeneration. Only upon this basis can a new and permanent ideal society be erected, such a society as will correspond with what Christ called the kingdom of God. This does not mean that Calvinists cannot cooperate with others in obtaining temporary social reforms. In the Netherlands they voted with the socialists and other groups in parliament for old age pensions, unemployment insurance and other social legislation. But when the socialists hope to create a new and perfect social order without the supernatural power of the Christian religion then the Calvinists tell them very frankly that this is only a dream. The fact is that many of the socialists have abandoned this dream. Because it takes sin as seriously as it does, Calvinism does not hope for an ideal society, a society without any social and economic evils, in this present age. *But this does not imply that we*

have no duty in the present order. The fact that we
cannot make it what it ought to be (for the simple
reason that the majority of men will not cooperate on
the basis of a revealed and supernatural gospel) does
not mean that we cannot make it far better than it is.
It is foolish, and even perverse, to say that we are not
going to do *anything* because we cannot accomplish
everything! Because we cannot make the world *ideal*
is no reason why we should not fight greed and graft
in politics, and injustice in the economic order. Our
faith in the sovereignty of God compels us to proclaim
that sovereignty in every sphere of life. In the measure that we recognize the sovereignty of God and the
stewardship of man we shall remedy and perhaps even
remove some of the gross evils from which we suffer
today. We cannot cure all disease, but a surgical operation may add ten years of health to the patient's life.
To eliminate all greed from our economic life is impossible in the midst of a sinful race, prone to all evil,
but satisfactory old age pensions and unemployment
insurance and a decent income for every honest man
are reforms which we can bring about if we have the
will to do it. *This is sound Calvinism!*

The Profit Motive and Monopolies.

Now let us apply these principles to some of our
modern economic problems.

Let us apply them first of all to the *profit motive.*
Sombart says that "Capitalism is motivated by the desire for profit. Hope of profit is the very soul of the
system. No matter how large the profits, they can never

reach a level sufficient to satisfy the spirit of capitalism." Prof. Ryskamp says the same thing, as I have
already indicated. Prof. F. W. Taussig, Professor of
Economics in Harvard University, says in his two-vol-
ume book *Principles of Economics:* "The aim of
the business man is to make money, and the chief motive which stirs him to making it is social ambition.
The successful business man is the backbone of the
well-to-do and possessing classes of modern society. His
ambition is to accumulate, not merely to earn a living.
The lawyer, the physician, the teacher, is reasonably
content if he succeeds in supporting and rearing a
family according to the standards of his class, and in
making some moderate provisions for the future; tho,
being in close association with the business set, he may
be infected also with the fever of accumulation. But
the business man cannot escape that infection. The
aim of all in his class is to gain more than enough
for support . . . The desire for wealth which possesses
the business class is thus not a simple motive, but one
very complex. It is much to be wished that other and
nobler motives could be substituted, and that the same
courage, judgment, strenuous work could be brought
to bear for rewards with a different sort and with less
unwelcome consequences in the inequalities of worldly
possessions." (p. 175 ff.)

At first sight it would seem as if this profit motive
of which we have been speaking is wholly bad, and
hence to be condemned in the light of our Calvinistic
principle of stewardship. But the profit motive need
not always be bad. If no advantage is taken of the

public, of the mass of consumers, and if living wages and perhaps better are paid to the employees, then one cannot say that the profit motive is sordid. But unfortunatly such and ideal situation is the exception in our modern economic life. Too much of our modern economic life is dominated solely by the profit motive, and all other motives are brushed aside as impractical. Men fail to recognize the sovereignty of God and their own stewardship. And we do not hesitate to say that Calvin would condemn most of our modern economic life as sordid, unchristian, in conflict with the principle of stewardship, because "the hope of profit is the very soul of the system." The motive is *not* the production of goods to satisfy human needs, but the accumulation of profits for the honor and pleasure and power that goes with this accumulation.

It is inevitable that the sordid profit motive should also be accompanied with *the monopoly of natural resources*, for natural resources are the fountain of wealth. When we speak of natural resources — mines, oil-wells, timber-lands, etc. — we are not thinking of private property. Calvin made it very clear in his opposition to the Libertines that private property is a Scriptural concept. A man has a right to own food, clothing, his own home and household goods, and also those things without which he cannot perform his daily toil. *But it should be remembered that even this right is not an absolute right.* There is no such thing as absolute ownership save in the case of God the Creator. What a man owns he may use for himself, but he may never use it in such a way that he injures others. As a steward he is also bound to use his property, in so far as he can, for the good of others. And this same principle surely applies to the natural resources, and all the more so because we are all dependent upon these natural resources. No man or group of men has the right to monopolize the natural resources. *They may be privately owned, but they are to be used and developed for the good of all.* Monopolies were already condemned by Calvin in his day, and these were relatively small monopolies compared with the vast aggregations of wealth today.

Dr. Colijn also refers to this subject in his *Toelichting* and I would like to quote him in the Dutch, following this with a translation. Says Dr. Colijn: "In de voor Israel geldende voorschriften moet de *algemeene* gedachte, die er in ligt, dus zorgvuldig worden opgespoord. En dan kan niet worden betwit, dat de Mozaische wetgeving er kennelijk naarstreeft *te scherpe* tegenstellingen en conflicten tusschen de volksgenooten te voorkomen. Vanuit *dit* beginsel geeft zij dan allerlei regelingen ook voor de eigendoms- en arbeidsverhoudingen. De economische zwakkere moet beschermd worden. Ook hij moet zijn roeping kunnen vervullen. Dientengevolge houdt de Israelietische wetgeving beginselen in, die bij het sluiten van arbeidscontracten in acht zijn te nemen. Zij bevat voorschriften omtrent rusttijden en vrije dagen, betreffende de uitbetaling van loon en het nemen van rente. Schrille armoede tracht zij de voorkomen. Het beschikkingsrecht over den eigendom, speciaal over het land, wordt op verschillende wijzen, ten bate van den arme, van de weduwe, en den wees bewerkt . . . " (etc., p. 405.)

We must diligently try to discover, says Dr. Colijn in the above quotation, the *universal* truth in the ordinances given to Israel. It cannot be denied that the object of this Mosaic legislation is to prevent sharp conflicts between the members of the commonwealth. Hence the laws regarding the ownership of property and labor conditions. The economically weaker members must be protected. They must be able to fulfill their calling. The result is that we find in the Hebrew legislation principles which we should observe today in the making of labor contracts. There are also laws in regard to periods of rest and holidays, the payment of wages and the taking of interest. This legislation was designed to prevent poverty. The ownership of property, especially of land, was regulated in several ways for the benefit of the poor, the widow and the orphan. Doubtless Dr. Colijn had in mind such passages as the following::

And the land shall not be sold in perpetuity; for the land is mine . . . and in all the land of your possession ye shall grant a redemption for the land. If thy brother be waxed poor, and sell some of his possession, then shall his kinsman that is next unto him come and shall redeem that which his brother hath sold . . . Lev. 25:23.

Thou shalt not oppress a hired servant that is poor and needy . . . in his day thou shalt give him his hire . . . thou shalt not wrest the justice due to the sojourner, or to the fatherless, nor take the widow's raiment to pledge . . . when thou repayest thy harvest in thp field, and hast forgot a sheaf in the field, thou shalt not go again to fetch it: it shall be for the sojourner, the fatherless, and for the widow, that Jehovah thy God may bless thee in all the work of thy hand . . . Deut. 24:14.

All this implies that the ownership of the land and of natural resources *is never an absolute ownership.* The owners always had to use their land for the good of all. Men must always realize that they are *stewards* of all that they own. This scriptural and Calvinistic principle is only too often forgotten by our modern corporations who use the vast natural resources they control for their own aggrandizement, regardless of the wages they pay their employees and regardless of the rights of multitudes of consumers.

It is this sinful failure to practice stewardship which also gives rise to the conflict between capital and labor. The laborer is divorced from the instruments of production, and unless he cooperates with his fellow-laborers he is the victim of the powerful corporations. Referring to the guilds of the late Middle Ages, Colijn writes that Christianity encouraged the organization of the various groups in society. He also reminds us that Kuyper always pleaded for the organization of labor. He calls the "freedom" which the non-unionist talks about *industrial slavery.*

Industrial Democracy.

The conflict between capital and labor naturally suggests a consideration of the merits of what is known as *industrial democracy*. In industrial democracy we have the *cooperation* of capital and labor instead of harsh conflict, and there is naturally far more opportunity for the operation of the principle of stewardship. Industrial democracy is something that has actually been tried and found very successful. Under this plan both the employer and the employees are represented in a board whose members are elected by the two groups. The employers provide most of the capital, sometimes all the capital, and the employers provide the labor, but in the board the rights of both groups are carefully safeguarded. Hart, Schaffner and Marx, the famous manufacturers of men's clothing, entered into such an agreement in 1916, and have found in this agreement a solution of their industrial problems. In the preamble of the agreement we read: "The parties to this pact realize that the interests sought to be reconciled herein will tend to pull apart, but they enter it in the faith that by the exercise of the co-operative and constructive spirit it will be possible to bring and to keep them together. This will involve as an indispensable pre-requisite the total suppression of the militant spirit by both parties and the development of reason instead of force as the rule of action. It will require also mutual consideration and concession, a willingness on the part of each party to regard and serve the interests of the other, so far as it can be done without too great a sacrifice of principle or interest. With this attitude assured it is believed no differences can arise which the joint tribunal cannot mediate and resolve in the interest of co-operation and harmony."

Mr. James Mullenbach, who died in the spring of 1935, was the chairman for some years of the arbitration board erected under this joint agreement, and he assured the writer that this agreement had been found very satisfactory by both sides.

Other industries have also experimented with this plan and found it very successful. In some cases the employees invest part of their wages in the stock and eventually become joint owners of the industry. Under such an arrangement they have the benefit of bigger profits in prosperous times and they take the losses of the industry in a better spirit in bad times, and at all times they are sure of their position provided they fulfill their part of the contract. And every employee is under a greater compulsion to fulfill his obligations because he hurts not only the employer but also his fellow-employees and himself if he does not.

I have discussed the plan both with employers and with social reformers. Some of the former object on the ground that they do not like to share the control of their industry with labor. And some of the social reformers object to the plan because it is too dependent on human good-will and they hold that nothing less than state control or state ownership will compel the industrial leaders to recognize the rights of the laboring class and of the public.

Dr. Colijn discusses the scheme in his *Toelichting*, and is very much in favor of it. It recognizes the Calvinistic principle of the antonomy of industry. prevents industry from being swallowed up and perhaps injured by an all-powerful state, and at the same time

it provides for the operation of the Calvinistic principle of stewardship. He devotes several pages to this
subject. He says:

"Er is in de maatschappij zelf metterdaad een
terugwijken van het individualisme, een *groeien* van de
solidariteitsgedachte, een streven naar organisatie van
het bedrijfsleven . . . De zaken van loon en arbeidstijd,
van leerlingwezen en verschillende sociale voorzieningen
zijn zaken die het geheele vak, het gansche bedrijf
aangaan. Zij moeten zooveel mogelijk, *collectief*
geregeld worden . . . Bij dit station willen we evenwel
niet stilstaan. Het einddoel is, dat er komt een alle
ondernemingen in een bedrijfstak omvattende organisatie, waarin patroons en arbeiders *samenwerken* en den
bloei van het bedrijf pogen te bevorderen. De mili-
tante tegenstelling tusschen werkgevers en arbeiders
behoort weggenomen te worden. En aan de arbeiders
mag een zekere rechtspositie in het bedrijf, waarin zij
werksaam zijn, niet worden onthouden." Dr. Colijn
makes it very clear that he favors such an organization
of capital and labor as will give both groups and all
concerned in the industry a proper and harmonious control over the industry. In other words, he favors what
we call in America *industrial democracy*. And this
would certainly be a development in harmony with our
Calvinistic social and economic principles.

Under such a development it is possible to con-
ceive of an industry, say the shoe industry, being opera-
ted by men with capital to invest in the industry, by
the managers who receive salaries, by the workers who
receive wages, and in some measure by the general

public that has some one in the board to represent and safeguard the consumers' interest. This is an altogether different thing from state socialism or communism of the Russian type, State Socialized Capitalism, and yet it provides for the cooperation of all interested in the production and distribution of shoes. It would provide for the greatest operation of our Calvinistic principle of stewardship.

It is conceivable — and this is also Dr. Colijn's point of view — that such an industrial development would call for *only a minimum* of state control or supervision, which, from our Calvinistic view-point, is a desirable thing.

Government Ownership or Supervision ?

The last problem that I will touch upon is that of *the relation of the state to the economic life.*

In view of the amazing growth in recent years of the totalitarian state we ought to thank God for our Calvinistic principle of the autonomy of the social and economic life.   In that monumental work of Dr. Abraham Kuyper, the three-volume *Gemeene Gratie,* this Calvinist more than thirty years ago clearly enunciated the important principle of the autonomy of the home, the church, the school, and the economic life. In chap. 11, vol. III, he speaks of "De Overheid en het Volk," and among other things so worthy of our attention today he says: "Er is dus niets van aan, dat de overheid heel ons leven zou overspannen en op eigen gezag heel one leven zou hebben te regelen. Integendeel, en persoonlijk, en in ons gezin, en in de maatschappij leven we een eigen zelfstanding leven; en over zulk een volk, dat alzoo in het bezit van een eigen leven is, treedt nu de overheid op, om een *beperkte en bepaalde,* haar opgedragen, taak te vervullen. De overheid mag zich dus volstrekt niet alles veroorlooven. Er zijn dingen die ze doen moet en mag. Maar er zijn ook dingen die haar niet vrijstaan. Tusschen haar leven en het leven der maatschappij liggen *grenzen,* en die grenzen heeft ze te eerbiedigen. En datgene wat het volk, en de enkele personen in dat volk, als eigen levensexistentite bezit, vormt dan de *rechten* en *vrijheden* van dat volk, die met hand en tand tegenover elke machtsoverschrijding der Overheid te verdedigen zijn." (All the italics are those of Kuyper.)

In the above quotation Dr. Kuyper says that it is not true at all that the government should control our whole life. On the contrary, in all spheres of life, the family, the social and economic orders, education and science, we should live our own life, with this understanding that the state will not allow the one individual to encroach upon the rights of the other, or the one sphere to dominate over the other sphere. There are duties which the state must perform in the midst of society, but there are also *limits* to its authority and those limits must be observed by the state. The encroachments of the state upon *the rights of the people* must be resisted at all costs.

This is a sound principle and one that should never be lost sight of, especially not today. We already have too many dictators like Lenin, Stalin, Mussolini, Hitler, and other would-be dictators. Too many

people are not aware of the dangers to our precious
liberties that lurk in fascism and state socialism. In
July, 1935, *The Presbyterian Tribune* printed a feature article under the caption "Fascism Threatens
the Church," in which there was much food for serious
thought. In defining fascism the writer said: "It is
necessary to be quite clear in our definition. And we
can be quite clear because fascism is a very clear,
specific, and strongly-marked phenomenon. Politically,
fascism is the totalitarian state whose motto is, 'Render
unto Ceasar *all things*,' presided over by a dictator
whose word is both the law and the prophets, and under
which, in the name of unity, order, efficiency, demo-
cratic representation is abolished and all civil liberties
abrogated. On the economic side, fascism is the last
desperate effort of a decaying capitalist order to defend
itself against complete disintegration and the revolt of
the masses. It seeks to accomplish this by using the
political power to enforce a measure of industrial discipline and to surpress every radical and liberal threat
to the capitalist order. Emotionally, fascism is the
use of any prejudice, fear, or unreasoned emotion by
which the people can be moved to support the dictatorship. Racial, religious, and national antipathies are
always deliberately accentuated by fascism." Says this
same writer: "People who do not think clearly are
likely to assume that a dictatorship in America would
necessarily mean the end of all democracy. No dictator who knows his business will permit any editor,
preacher, politician, or ordinary citizen so much as to
whisper his opposition. The conclusion of the matter

is well described by the vicar in one of H. G. Wells' novels: 'My church is done. My God has been dropped again. There is another God now, the State, the State Almighty. I tell you that God will be worse than Moloch. You had better keep that in mind. It has no vision, only expediency. It has no morality, only power, and it will have no arts, for it will punish the free spirit with death.' "

Will fascism come to America? Dr. Charles Clayton Morrison tried to answer this question in an editorial in *The Christian Century* in July, 195. In his opinion the signs of something very much similar to fascism are already here. And the writer of the article from which the above quotation was made answers the question in the following fashion: "Let me briefly cite reasons why we should rid ourselves of the comfortable assurance that something like this cannot happen in America.

"1. The enormous success of such an organization as the Ku Klux Klan is certainly no assurance that we are not capable of the mad racial propaganda of an Adolph Hitler.

"2. We have already in this country five organizations either openly asking for a dictator or pursuing tactics which lead to the same result. One is not at all certain that the American Legion would not provide a large following for a fascist movement.

"3. Commendation of European dictators who flaunt democracy but preserve capitalism and approval of undemocratic suppression of radicals prove that the first love of large numbers is not democracy but the present economic order. They are essentially fascist in that they wish, at all costs, to see this order perpetuated.

"4. Bills have been introduced in many state legislatures, as well as in the national congress, which constitute the first step toward the fascist state. Aimed ostensibly at communism, these bills, if enacted, would provide the legal basis for the suppression of all liberal and radical activity and opinion."

Says this writer in conclusion: "The time to fight for liberty is before we lose it. The Church's peculiar stake in the present trend toward fascism lies in the circumstance that if the trend is not checked we shall one day discover, like the churches of Germany, that a pagan state is capable of anything."

Communism is no less an enemy of our Calvinistic democracy. Marx, Engels and other outstanding nineteenth century communists did not believe in democracy and in a parliamentary system of government with all groups and interests in society represented in the parliament or national congress. Only the "workers," the proletariat, should rule. And the communists of Russia are putting this principle into practice. People who do not believe in communism, no matter how peaceable their behavior may be, are regarded as enemies of the government, and are in danger of being ruthlessly suppressed. The leaders of Russia justify their suppression of the opposition, and of free speech and of a free press, on the ground that "communism is fighting for its life," and if the critics of communism are allowed to survive they will be a menace to the very existence of the communist regime. "It is a war to the finish" say Stalin and his crowd, and no mercy can be shown to people who do not support the communist state. There need never be any shadow of doubt in our mind that if the communists got control of the American government they would suppress all free speech, all criticism of the communist government and its policies. Democracy as we have known it, and as propagated and defended by all genuine Calvinists, would be a thing of the past — at least, until the spirit of the Beggars, the Huguenots and Puritans would once more take possession of the souls of men. While every form of communism is not to be identified with the despotic Russian communism, it is a fact that the communism generally propagated in America is of the Russian type and therefore should be opposed by every genuine Calvinist and lover of human freedom. The communism of dictator Stalin of Russia means the end of American freedom.

More Government Control

The Calvinist's opposition to an all-powerful state of the Russian or German type does not mean, however, that he does not realize the great need of *government control* over large areas of business and industry to curb our growing economic evils. While opposed to the government *ownership* of the means of production, because he believes in a certain amount of independence in every sphere of life, and holds that it is not the task of the state to produce food and clothing, at the same time he never forgets that we are living in an abnormal society. In the kind of world in which we are living men tend in the economic life to seize and monopolize power and riches, and therefore for the good of all it behooves society through the organ of the state to curb the wicked passions of men. We need laws to prevent food monopolies and other monopolies of the essentials of human existence; laws to regulate wages and hours, and in many cases also prices. Why take advantage of the labor glut and comply men to work for scandalously low wages? The day after the United States Supreme Court declared the NRA unconstitutional, some of the department stores in Chicago announced to their employees that they should prepare to work an hour longer the next day — without extra pay, of course. It is a fact that there are men who will not pay a living wage unless compelled to do so. They ought to do so of their own accord, and because they realize that they are stewards of God, or, at least because they have sufficient sense of justice to feel that the laborer is worthy of his hire. But many will not.

We need laws to regulate child labor. With millions of able-bodied men out of work, fathers of dependent families, why should boys and girls in their early teens work on the hot fields and in factories and stores? Since the NRA was declared unconstitutional, and the New York law raising the minimum age for full-time employment for children in their teens does not go into effect until September, 1936, there has been a tremendous increase in that state in the number of permits issued to children who are 14 and 15 years old, which indicates that younger children are taking the jobs which in 1934, and early in 1935, were given to older boys and girls. If there are no laws to protect the children, they are exposed to the cruel mercies of unscrupulous employers and hard-pressed parents. To be sure, there are many employers, possibly the majority, who see the injustice of employing young children, but they also are at the mercy of the unprincipled group. Competition being as keen as it is, they are ofttimes compelled to employ the cheapest labor. Many of them would welcome laws to protect the children and to enable them to do the thing dictated by their own conscience.

We need laws to prevent millions of *married women,* whose husbands are making good wages, occupying the jobs of fathers of dependent families. As it is today, there are many married couples who refuse to have children for no other reason than that *both* may work and that they may enjoy the luxury of a double income. We need laws to prevent such an injustice. This does not mean that just as soon as a woman marries she must be thrown out of her job. This may be an injustice to her and to her husband, and possibly to parents or a widow that are receiving part of her income. But the evil that must be curbed by leislation is that multitudes of married women *have taken over the jobs that were once held by married men because they were willing to work for less wages.*

We need laws to prevent unemployment. It is a well-known fact that many industries discharge a large number of employees after they have had them less than five years for no other reason than that they can hire new men for less money. The writer can mention the names of firms that do this thing systematically.

We need laws to provide for unemployment and sickness insurance, and old-age pensions. Unemployment is so frequent in our modern industrial set-up that the average man cannot save enough money to tide him and his family over the period when he has no work. Sickness insurance is also needed. And old age pensions in a day when men cannot find a job after forty, and consequently their earning power is limited to a few years, is simply a matter of social justice. This pension should be large enough to provide for a decent living. It need not be two hundred dollars a month, but it should cover a man's actual needs.

We need these and many other laws, and no intelligent Christian will condemn these things as "socialistic". Workmen's compensation laws were once condemned as socialistic, but we all believe in them today. Legislation of this type may save us from a revolution with all its chaos, and with all the danger of putting fascism or communism into power. It may also save us from that state socialism which would make the state the absolute owner of our farms and industries and all our other economic activities. It will mean *private ownership,* and considerable room for *personal initiative,* but with a *governmental check on the sinful passions of men.* This is good Calvinism. And, of course, it is good Christianity.

V.

CONCLUSION

ALL THIS must finally bring us to the conclusion that our economic problems resolve themselves in their deeper aspects into ethical and religious problems. That is not saying that there is more chance of the Christian theologians and Christian philosophers solving them than the economists. But it does mean that if the economists are to solve them they must reckon with the ethical nature of man and the ethical implications of the economic life. Our economic life suffers from *the curse of sin,* and only when we reckon with that tremendous fact and accept the way of salvation offered in the Gospel can we begin to live in harmony with the divine ordinances for the economic life and thus promote the economic well-being of man. Our duty then as Calvinists is to denounce the terrible evils in our economic life as sin before God, sin which if not repented of will end in the judgments so vividly set forth in Revelation 18 — that chapter in which the seer of Patmos describes the economic life of the last days and cries out as he sees *Babylon,* symbol of the economic life, perishing in her sins: "Woe, woe, the great city, Babylon, the strong city: for in one hour is thy judgment come. And the merchants of the earth weep and mourn over her, for no man buyeth

their merchandise any more; merchandise of gold and
silver and pearls and fine linen and silk, and ointment
and wine and oil and fine flour and wheat and cattle
and sheep . . . and slaves . . . and *the souls of men.*"

The longer we ponder upon our economic problems
the more clearly we see that the economic problems are
ethical problems, that is, problems that concern the
ethical attitudes of men. And for that very reason no
minister of the gospel has the right to ignore them.
While it would be foolish to substitute lectures on economics for the preaching of the Word of God, we must
bring that Word of God to bear upon the economic
life of the people. They have no right to justify their
unchristian practices in the business world or in industrial life by saying that "business is business," and that
the duty of the minister is to preach the "simple gospel." There are only too many people in our own
churches who think that the sole purpose, or at least
the chief purpose, of the gospel is to offer us comfort
in the hour of death, but that it has no message at all
for our daily life as we struggle to make a living. Our
Lord taught us very definitely to pray, "Thy will be
done on earth," *on the earth on which we are living
right now,* in all of life's relationships, and these certainly include our relationships in the social, economic
and political life. No man who knows the history
of the past 1900 years will ever deny that only too often
the church has failed to follow in the footsteps of the
great prophets of Israel in their vigorous denunciation
of selfishness and exploitation in the economic life.
This preaching is not popular with our people, especi-

ally not with those who have prospered under an un-righteous economic system. In a sermon in Grand Rapids a few years ago, long before I went to Chicago, I said that men had no right to monopolize all of the resources of God's good earth. I said that these practices stood condemned in the light of the eighth commandment, and I also mentioned some of the unethical practices of our own people. After the sermon a successful business man told me that he thought the preachers ought to "stick to the gospel." There are only too many people like that in our own churches and some of us cater to them, and still make ourselves believe that we are preaching the whole counsel of God. If ever a child of God rejoiced in his heavenly heritage it was John Calvin, but while he was in Geneva from 1540 to the day of his death he brought the impact of the gospel to bear upon every phase of the life of that city, and when he died Geneva was the best governed city in all Europe. Calvin never could preach a gospel which was an opium for the consciences of business men who practiced cut-throat competition or of employers who take advantage of the labor glut. Once more I quote this word of Calvin, speaking of the advantage the rich take of the poor in times of unemployment, "That is what the rich often do — they spy out occasions to cut down the wages of the poor by half when they have no employment." That is not socialism. Nor is it communism. It is Calvinism. It is a protest against social injustice from the lips of one whose motto was *Coram Deo.*

What the times demand is the very message that

Calvinism offers, Calvinism with its emphasis on the sovereignty of God, the stewardship of man, and the Holy Spirit as the source of power to do the will of a sovereign God in the service of our neighbor. Democracy is in peril. It may perish sooner than we think. Hitler says that Germany will lead the world out of darkness into light, which means that the world must adopt fascism! And here in America synods and conferences and religious leaders are pleading for a new world order, and many of the people vote for the resolutions framed by their leaders without the least idea what they mean by a new world order.

We believe that we have an adequate Christ because we accept the whole revelation of God, the letters of Paul as well as the Sermon on the Mount. We have a gospel which is still the power of God unto salvation. But what we perhaps lack is a profound insight into the implications of that Word of God for the whole of life, also for our business world. Paul saw the world of his day as a world that was lying in wickedness, that was alienated from God, without Christ, and without hope. We need nothing less than this profound insight into the degeneracy of our times.

But lest we should appear to be preachers of despair—prophets of gloom—we must proclaim with heaven-born enthusiasm and in fresh pentecostal power the unsearchable riches of Christ. One thing is sure, this generation has tried everything, from theosophy and spiritism to humanism and atheism, and is weary of it all. Says John Dewey, our greatest social philosopher: "The chief characteristic of the present age is its despair of any constructive philosophy, not just in its technical meaning, but in the sense of an integrated outlook and attitude . . . The result is disillusionment." And James Truslow Adams writes: "We are floundering in a morass . . . We are bewildered." How remarkable that our greatest leaders of thought should make such honest confessions. If the world does not know the way out, then let us with renewed zeal and enthusiasm, and in humble dependence upon the Holy Spirit, follow Him who said:

"I am the Way, the Truth, and the Life."

When men turn toChrist, they find GOD, and finding God, they find one another in a nobler and more harmonious social life.

BIBLIOGRAPHY

BAVINCK, H. — *Versamelde Opstellen.*

BRUNNER, H. E. — The Theology of Crisis (Barthianism).

CALVIN, JOHN — Institutes and Commentaries.

CHALMERS, THOMAS — Political Economy.

COLIJN, H. — *Toelichting op het Antirevolutionair Beginsel-program.* (Indispensable for a knowledge of present-day economic Calvinism).

DIEPENHORST, P. A. — *Het Socialisme.*

GILLEN AND BLACKMAR — Outlines of Sociology.

GILLEN, J. L. — Social Pathology.

HARKNESS, GEORGIA — John Calvin, The Man and his Ethics.

KUYPER, ABRAHAM — Gemeene Gratie.

KUYPER, ABRAHAM — *Gemeene Gratie.*

MANGOLD, G. B. — Social Pathology.

MARSHALL, L. C. — Industrial Society.

PROPERTY — A Symposium by British Writers. (Very valuable.)

SMITH, ADAM — The Wealth of Nations.

TAUSSIG, F. W. — Principles of Economics.

WALLACE, H. A. — Statesmanship and Religion.

GIVE ME NEITHER POVERTY NOR RICHES*

*Give me neither poverty nor riches; feed me with
food that is needful for me: lest I be full, and deny
thee, and say, Who is Jehovah? Or lest I be poor, and
steal, and use profanely the name of my God.*
PROV. 30:8, 9.

THE BIBLE is a remarkable book. It touches every
phase of life, not only the life of the spirit, but also
the life of the body. It is like godliness, profitable unto
all things, having the promise of the life that now is
and that which is to come. It teaches us how to live
in this world and how to prepare for the next. It exhorts us to earn our daily bread and it admonishes us
to seek the bread that will never perish, the bread that
came down from heaven, even our Lord Jesus Christ,
Who said of Himself, "I am the bread of life: if any
man eat of this bread he shall live forever."

In our text we have a most unusual prayer. "Give
me neither poverty nor riches; feed me with the food
that is needful for me: lest I be full and deny Thee,
and say, Who is Jehovah? Or lest I be poor, and steal,
and use profanely the name of my God."

1. This child of God prays that he may *not be
rich.* "Give me neither poverty nor riches." That
certainly is an unusual prayer . Give me neither riches.

There are very few people who pray a prayer like

* A Sermon Preached in the Second Christian Reformed Church,
Englewood, Chicago, Ill.

93

this. If it is a sincere prayer it implies that this man does not desire to be rich. And even though he should desire it, he realizes that it is not good for him to be rich and so he prays, Give me . . . Now there are very few people who do not desire to be rich. Riches are a source of power. You can do so much more if you are rich. You can have so much more if you are rich, a beautiful home, beautiful furniture, beautiful clothes, a Packard or a Rolls-Royce car. You can have more comforts, more luxuries more ease. And in normal times less worries. The man who has only an ordinary income is troubled by the grim spectre of unemployment, sickness or old age. It is only natural that most people should desire riches, or at least to have more than they have.

It is possible that many of us are not conscious of this desire; that we never say to ourselves, "O that I were rich!" And it may be that most of us are thoroughly convinced by this time that we shall never be rich and that it is useless to desire to be rich. We have reconciled ourselves to what we regard as the inevitable.

But the true child of God goes farther than this. He realizes that it is not even desirable to be rich. It is better not to be rich. Give me neither poverty nor riches. Do not give me riches.

It is sometimes said that it is a good thing to be rich because it enables us to do so much more for others, for people in need, and for the kingdom of God. I have heard noble and generous people say, "I wish that I were rich so that I could do far more good in the world. This cause needs money and that cause needs money, if I were rich how much more good I could do." The people who say this thing undoubtedly mean what they say, and yet even in their case it is a question whether they would be better off if they were rich. Occasionally a generous man becomes rich and he develops into such a stingy miser that it is a pity he ever became rich. The more a man has the more he wants. There is something fascinating about money, wealth. It takes hold of a man and begets in him the desire for more and more.

The child of God who knows himself will be more likely to pray, "Give me neither poverty nor riches *lest I be full and deny thee.* Less I be full because of my riches, satisfied with my riches, and no longer feel the need of God. I know, O my God, it ought never to be so. It ought not to be possible for riches to supplant Thee in my affections. But I have seen it happen with others. And I know that I am prone to fall into sin and to deny Thee. And so I pray, Give me not riches, lest I should be full and deny Thee."

We know very well that a man need not deny God because he is rich. Far from it. Abraham was very rich and we read that he was called the friend of God. Joseph of Arimathea was rich and yet he was not ashamed to give the Lord Jesus a decent, even an honorable burial. Christ never condemned the rich because they were rich. But He did warn them repeatedly of the dangers that are bound to accompany riches. "Lay not up for yourselves treasures on earth where

moth and rust doth corrupt . . ." "A man's life con-
sisteth not in the abundance of things which he possesses.

Riches are apt to lead to luxury and luxury to
vice. Many a man has led a godly and righteous life
until he got rich and then he fell into temptation, and
began to lead a very sinful life. I know a man who
was a regular attendant upon divine worship, a kind
father, a good husband, until he got rich, very rich;
and then began to associate with very worldly people,
fell in love with a worldly woman, got a divorce, and
to this day he has not returned to the righteous life
of his youth. I am sure if that man had never become
a millionaire, he would never have been caught in the
snares of his riches.

And even if wealth does not lead to luxury and to
vice, to marital unfaithfulness and to a divorce, it does
tend to make a man proud, independent of the Lord,
so that his religion and spiritual life suffers. Many
an earnest and sincere Christian has lost much of his
piety and devotion after being surrounded by the comforts and enjoying the pleasures that are so easy to
obtain when a man is wealthy. It is so easy to do what
you want, to get what you want when you are wealthy,
that we are in great danger of developing an independent spirit. "Give me not riches, lest I be full
and deny Thee and say, Who is Jehovah?"

II. But if it be perilous to be rich, it is also perilous to be poor. "Give me neither poverty nor riches,
lest I be full . . . or lest I be poor and steal, and use
profanely the name of my God."

No doubt there are children of God who can say: "No matter how poor I might become, I would not steal; I would rather starve than steal." And no doubt God can give His children grace not to steal. If a man is poor and hungry, and especially if his children are suffering want and he sees a chance to get what he needs he will be tempted to steal. A man who never thought of stealing, and who would have never stolen if he had not been in dire distress, may steal when hard pressed. When a man's children are crying for bread and there is no way of getting bread except by theft, the temptation to steal is almost irresistable. No wonder the child of God prays: "Give me not poverty lest I steal, and by my stealing profane the name of my God. I am known as a child of God, I have confessed His name, but if I steal I certainly am dishonoring the name of my God."

When a man is poor he is not only tempted to steal, to commit theft, but he is tempted to practice fraud and deception. He may not steal outright, but may resort to fraud and deception. He may lie or cheat or indulge in other questionable practices and thus dishonor the name of his God. People are so hard pressed for work nowadays that they do lie in order to get a job. They lie about their ability, their qualifications, their age, in order to get a job. And the fact that a man is refused a job because he is forty or fifty, as if a man of that age were not just as valuable as a man of thirty, also tends to make men lie

about their age. The pinch of poverty and the injustice of employers makes them liars.

Now it is true that we ought not to lie no matter
what our circumstances are, but human nature being
what it is, it is better to be kept out of temptation and
therefore the Christian prays: "Give me not poverty
lest I should sin against my God."

The widespread unemployment today is accompanied with many dangerous temptations, and a Christian may well pray that he may keep his employment
or that he may soon find employment.

As already said, there is the temptation to lie. Circumstances are such today that men are forced to lie in
order to get a job. Such a condition is bad, as bad
as can be. It tends to undermine the moral foundations of society, foundations which are in bad enough
shape already.

Secondly, men are tempted to buy a job, to resort
to corruption in order to get a job, which means that
the man who can offer the biggest bribe gets the job.
Men ought to be given a job because they can satisfy
the requirements of the position, not because they buy
the job. When jobs can be obtained through bribes,
then the man offering the biggest bribe gets the job,
but perhaps a poorer man is worthier, more capable
and in greater need of the job.

Another bad feature of our unemployment is that
many employers are tempted to take advantage of the
situation. They are taking on as few people as possible
and loading all the work on those few people, so that
they are actually over-worked. They are treated like

slaves. This is unjust to the people employed and unjust to those who need work. It is contrary to the law of Christ, "Thou shalt love thy neighbor as thyself."

And still another evil accompanying this widespread unemployment is that men are in danger of losing their faith and courage. Enforced idleness is a bad thing for a man's spiritual life. It makes him discouraged, pessimistic, and he gets disgusted with life and with everybody round about him. He gets disgusted with the church and the minister and the people of the church. It is a bad thing for a man's mental and spiritual life not to have anything to do day after day, and week after week.

And the worry that is bound to accompany unemployment is also a dangerous thing. When there is no food in the house, when the children are hungry and crying for bread, or when bills are piling up and there is no way of meeting these bills, a situation has been created which is dangerous for a man's mental and spiritual life. No matter how good a Christian he may be, he has so much to worry about that it hurts his spiritual life. Even then the Lord is able to uphold us, and to keep alive our faith and hope, for He is almighty and ever-faithful, but it is a dangerous situation.

III. Hence this prayer in our text is so appropriate for a time like this. "Give me neither poverty nor riches; feed me with the food that is needful for me . . . "

We have the right to pray for the things that we need for the body, for food and clothing and shelter.

The Lord has created us with a body, with bodily needs, and these must be supplied. Hence we have the right to pray, even the duty to pray, "Feed me with the food that is needful for me." I have heard people say that we ought to be so occupied with the things of the spirit, of the soul, of the kingdom of God, that we do not think of the body. But that is not a Scriptural attitude. We have been created with many physical needs and we may bring these needs before the Lord.

Did not Jesus teach us to pray, "Give us this day our daily bread"? He taught us to pray for the things that we need for the body.

And did He not feed the multitude with bread? When they were hungry he said to the disciples: "Give ye them to eat." And when the disciples were unable to give them bread He provided bread. What does it show? That He was considerate of their physical needs. Almost all of His miracles were miracles for the well-being of the body. "He knoweth our frame and remembereth that we are dust," made of the dust of the earth, and that we must live out of he earth. Hence the prayer, "Give us this day our daily bread." Hence the prayer in our text, "Feed me with the food that is needful for me," if I am to sustain this life and in this life serve Thee.

This is a prayer for WORK, for EMPLOYMENT, for a divine blessing upon our toil so that we may have food, and everything else that is needed for the body. The author of our text certainly did not expect to receive his food in a miraculous fashion. What he prays for is that he may have health and strength and opportunity to work, and thus may have the food which he need. Nowhere does the Scripture teach that we are to have our food *without working*.

That we are to *work for our food* follows from our creation in the image of God. God is not an inactive, unproductive being, but the most energetic being in the universe, the source of all life and energy, and being created in His image we are intended to be working and productive beings. Therefore we also read: "Six days shalt thou work and do all labor." It is just as much a duty to work during the week as it is a duty to rest on the Sabbath. And the apostle Paul wrote to the idle Thessalonians: "He that will not work shall not eat." In keeping with this ordinance of the Lord the author of our text does not pray that he may have food without working, food without effort, but that he may be so blessed in his work and have the food he needs, and all othr things that are needed for the body.

And that is certainly a much-needed prayer today, the prayer that we hay have *work, employment,* and thus may have food . . .

The man of self-respect, and especially the Christian, does not care to be supported by charity. If there is no work then he must be supported by charity for we may not allow our fellowmen to starve. But that is not normal, and is far from desirable. It is contrary to the divine ordinance that we should work six days and thus support ourselves. Charity, relief, doles for able-bodied men and women must always be regarded as abnormal and highly undesirable. What we

need and must have is *work, employment,* so that all
who are able to work may find work, and thus have an
answe rto this beautiful prayer: "Feed me with the food
that is needful for me."

This situation in which we find ourselves today,
namely, that millions of people are able to work and
eager to work, and yet unable to find work, is a *curse.*
It may be a curse due to our own folly, our own greed
to the mistakes made in recent years, but it is a curse
none the less, and we are all suffering from it, in one
way or another. If one member in the body suffers,
says Paul, the whole body suffers. And that is true
of human society. Millions of members in the social
body are in distress and we are all suffering.

There are deep-seated evils in modern society which
must be corrected or our civilization will crash to
pieces. A few years ago many men were working over-
time, and on Saturday night they were so tired out that
they were not fit to go to church on Sunday morning,
which means that a man's spiritual life suffers under
such conditions, and this is one of the reasons why
the church and the pulpit are interested in social problems. Today the situation is exactly the reverse. A
man cannot buy a job. Hence what we need is such
a management of society, such economic planning as
will make employment more regular so that the average
family may have the food it needs from day to day.

Another evil of our time is that when a man is forty
or fifty years he is tossed upon the economic junk pile
as so much waste! Think of it, men with brain and

brawn, at the very best period of life, with years of experience and knowledge to their credit, told to go home because they are not needed any longer in our economic set-up! The motive too often for this discharge of older employees is the opportunity of employing new men or younger men at lower wages. The motive is no other than greed.

All of which reminds us that our greatest need in the social order is Christ with the atoning sacrifice which reconciles God and man and imparts the motive and power for unselfish service, and thus provides the foundation for a more just social order. And in the measure that we preach Christ and live Christ, and win new converts for Christ, we are bringing our social order a little nearer the ideal of our Lord and Master, Who said, "I am not come to be ministered unto, but to minister and to give my life a ransom for many." Conditions in the social order can improve and will improve as larger numbers of Christians apply the teachings of our divine Lord to the problems of our day. Christ is the Light of the world, also the Light that illumines and transforms the social order.